A STEP BY STEP GUIDE TO PROFITABLE POULTRY FARMING FOR LOCAL CONSUMPTION AND EXPORT.

An invaluable guide for farmers in poultry farming business.

POULTRY BUSINESS MANUAL

ALL RIGHTS RESERVED

POULTRY OPERATIONS

A STEP BY STEP GUIDE TO PROFITABLE POULTRY FARMING FOR LOCAL CONSUMPTION AND EXPORT.

An Invaluable guide for Farmers in Poultry Farming Business.

===POULTRY OPERATIONS ===

ALL RIGHTS RESERVED

Published by:

PHILIP NELSON INSTITUTE OF AGRICULTURAL RESEARCH.

Advancement of Agriculture through Research, Policy analysis and Education.

P.O BOX 55601 Falomo, Ikoyi, Lagos, Nigeria.

E-MAIL: philipnelsonassociates@yahoo.com, philipnelsoninstitute@yahoo.com

A STEP BY STEP GUIDE TO PROFITABLE POULTRY FARMING FOR LOCAL CONSUMPTION AND EXPORT.

THE SECRETS OF THE SUCCESSFUL POULTRY FARMERS.

An Invaluable Guide for Farmers in the Poultry Business.

COPYRIGHT

(c.) PHILIP NELSON INSTITUTE OF AGRICULTURAL RESEARCH.

ISBN NUMBER:

SPECIAL WARNING

No part of this publication may be reproduced or transmitted in any form or by any means without permission. It is a condition of the company that business training manuals supplied to any trainee remains the property of the company.

The trainee will not let any third party have access to it, either by lending, reselling or hireling. Unauthorized possession of this manual is illegal. In as much as this book is copyright, it may not be reproduced by any means, in whole or in part, without permission. Application with regard to copyright should be addressed to the publishers-

PHILIP NELSON INSTITUTE OF AGRICULTURAL RESEARCH.

PHILIP NELSON INSTITUTE OF AGRICULTURAL RESEARCH

Dispatch advice

Name of Client:_____

_____

Address of Client:_____

_____
_____

Tel:_____

E-mail:_____

Reference number:_____

This book is the poultry operations manual you requested for. Please quote your reference number in any correspondence with us to enable us trace your files and treat your request adequately. This form is duplicate. Complete the two forms ,copy out one and give us for our own documentation.

Thanks for your patronage.

-Management.

PHILIP NELSON INTITUTE OF AGRICULTURAL RESEARCH

Dispatch advice

Name of Client:_____

Address of Client:_____

_____

_____

_____

Tel:_____

E-mail:_____

Reference number:_____

_____

This book is the poultry operations manual that you requested for. Please quote your reference number in any correspondence with us to enable us trace your files and treat your request adequately.

This form is duplicate. Complete the two forms, copy out one, and give us for our own documentation.

Thanks for your patronage.

- Management.

NOTE TO THE READER

We are providing this service for the benefit of humanity, fellow men and the society. Our publications department has divided this report into 18 chapters of 3 parts.

They provides all the start-up information needed for the poultry farming business. We suggest that you read this manual carefully, make some notes and then re-read it for a complete understanding of the business. Many of the facts in it will not only be informative but surprising as well.

It is in this manual that we have spent our time and efforts and it is also in this manual that you are paying for.

This manual is a standard manual that we prepared for your convenience. It is designed to save you time and it contains primary instructions that every poultry farmer should know before opening any poultry business.

This poultry operations manual will show you not only what to do but how to do it.

If you learn and apply the simple basic poultry farming techniques revealed here, you will have mastered the secret of true and lasting success in poultry farming business.

The Publishers

PHILIP NELSON INSTITUTE OF AGRICULTURAL RESEARCH.

aPN PHILIP NELSON INSTITUTE OF AGRICULTURAL RESEARCH
Telephone: +234816582414, +2348140624643

E-mail: philipnelsoninstitute@yahoo.com

A STEP BY STEP GUIDE TO A PROFITABLE POULTRY FARMING BUSINESS FOR LOCAL CONSUMPTION AND EXPORT.

Hello,

My name is Philip Anochie. I am the President and CEO of Philip Nelson Institute of Agricultural Research- Your partner in crop and livestock farming. We are advancing agriculture through research, policy analysis and education.

I am here to introduce you to an international poultry farming business training manual titled: " A step by step guide to a profitable poultry farming business for local consumption and export".

This comprehensive poultry farming business training manual is an essential start-up procedure training for an individual that wants to go into poultry farming business.

It is also an invaluable guide for commercial poultry farmers already into chicken egg production and other aspects of poultry farming as it revealed the well-guarded secrets of successful commercial poultry farmers and exporters of poultry products worldwide.

This poultry farming business training manual is organized into 18 modules on poultry farming which consists of daily and weekly step-by-step procedures used in poultry farming operations to achieve the highest profit potential and also sources of loans to finance your poultry business.

WELL GUARDED SECRETS REVEALED

In the exciting world of poultry business, there are some well-guarded technical poultry farming secrets used by the old pros all built on sound scientific principles.

If you are looking for an easy to run business with a minimum of problems, poultry business could be ideal for you.

The result of our extensive research and experience in this business is now available. In actuality, this is a complete professional start-up and operational poultry business training manual covering such topics as:

PART ONE: PROFITABLE POULTRY PRODUCTION

CHAPTER 1: LITTER

CHAPTER 2: EGG PRODUCTION- THE MONEY SPINNER.

CHAPTER 3: CARING FOR DAY-OLD CHICKS.

CHAPTER 4: BROODING: Week 1.

DAY 1 – The day-old chicks history.

DAY 2 - Milk and Glucose treatment.

DAY 3 - Introducing the feed trough

DAY 4 - Culling day.

DAY 5 - Farm uniforms.

DAY 6 – Prevention of diseases.

DAY 7 - The end of the first week's programme.

CHAPTER 5 : BROODING CONTINUES

Week 2 - Room size and number of chicks.

Week 3 - Trace elements

Week 4 - Skimmed milk for treatment of fowl pox.

Week 5 – Debeaking

CHAPTER 6: REARING : Weeks 6-18

Week 6 - The grower period

Week 7 - Coccidiosis treatment

Week 8 - Sick Bay treatments

Week 9 - Resting week for hygiene.

Week 10- Newcastle diseases.

Week 11- Cleanliness.

Week 12- Treatment of colds

Week 13- Changing feeding habits

Week 14- Building weight

Week 15- Fowl pox

Week 16- Feeding , alternative method

Week 17- Green leaves in the feed (Trace elements).

Week 18- Aim at live weight of the birds.

CHAPTER 7: NEW LIGHT PROGRAMMES BEGINS

Week 34- The peak periods

Week 35- Feed needs vitamins

Week 36- Feed needs lime

Week 37- More carbohydrate and flint

Week 38- Feed less grain but more protein

Week 39- Add milk in the feed

Week 40- Check profit and records

Week 41- More market outlets

Week 42- Channels of distribution.

CHAPTER 9: Brooding 1000chicks or more for eggs?

CHAPTER 10: How to preserve eggs and save money.

PART TWO: COMMERCIAL BROILERS PRODUCTION

CHAPTER 11: BROILERS: Another money spinner.

(a) Organized production.

(b) Labour involved.

(c) Expenses.

CHAPTER 12: BROILERS: Planning for more profit all the year round.

CHAPTER 13: BROILERS: Maximum efficiency.

(a) Feed composition.

(b) Routine daily care.

CHAPTER 14: Turning hobby to business.

(a) Starting 100 broilers or more.

(b) Efficient production methods.

CHAPTER 15: REARING LARGER COCKERELS FOR PROFIT.

PART THREE: POULTRY DISEASES, MEDICATION AND VACCINES.

CHAPTER 16: Common poultry diseases.

CHAPTER 17: Established poultry medication and vaccines.

CHAPTER 18: Sources of Agricultural loans and many more.

Several successful poultry farmers were interviewed and questioned extensively by our institute, to provide a composite to the many proven and profitable operations to unearth any hidden reasons why they were more successful than the vast majority.

We reveal all their secrets in what is possible a little-known but very lucrative industry. Here is your chance to learn the real truth about this exciting business.

If you are looking for a perfect recession-proof part-time business you can run and still keep your job, poultry farming business is ideal for you.

Thanks for your patronage.

Philip I. Anochie

President/ CEO.

Philip Nelson Institute of Agricultural Research.

11, John Fayemi Close, Akesan Bus stop, LASU-Igando road, Alimosho LGA, Lagos state.

P.O.Box 55601 Falomo, Ikoyi, Lagos, 101008, Nigeria,

West Africa.

Telephone: Local: 08173175179, 08140624643, 081-6658-2414

International: +2348173175179, +2348140624643 +2348166582414

E-mail: philipnelsonassociates@yahoo.com

philipnelsoninstitute@yahoo.com

A STEP BY STEP GUIDE TO PROFITABLE POULTRY FARMING FOR LOCAL CONSUMPTION AND EXPORT

POULTRY FARMING BUSINESS MANUAL

ALL RIGHTS RESERVED

ISBN :

PUBLISHED BY

Philip Nelson Institute of Agricultural Research

P.O. BOX 55601 Falomo, Ikoyi, Lagos 101008 Nigeria.

E-mail: Philipnelsoninstitute@yahoo.com.

Tel: +2348166582414, +2348140624643.

INTRODUCTION AND BACKGROUND INFORMATION

This book contains information on poultry management which includes preparation of the litter, egg production, caring for day old chicks, brooding, rearing, light program, laying period, brooding 1000 chicks or more eggs, how to preserve eggs and save money, commercial broiler production, feed composition, routine day care, rearing large cockerels for profit, and common poultry diseases.

It also contains information on established poultry medication and vaccines, food consumption, skillful use of artificial light, planning for more profit all the year round, production all the year round, application of poultry vaccines and sample poultry farming business plan. At the end of this training, you will become a complete professional poultry farmer.

- **Philip Anochie.**

CHAPTER 1: THE LITTER

When you are starting poultry, the knowledge of litter comes first. A number of materials are suitable for deep litter, but some are more suitable than others. The main attributes of a litter are that it should be absorbent and as free from dust as possible. The following are used on their own or in combination with others, peat-moss, straw, chaff, cut straw, shavings, saw dust and wool shoddy.

1. PEAT –MOSS: This is very dusty and as such not recommended for the tropics. It is very absorbent and long lasting. Because it is dusty, the interior of the house tends to be covered with a fine brown dust. It is dark and does not reflect light. A good grade peat-moss with as little dust in it as possible, should always be used.
2. SAW DUST: It extensively used because of its quality and beauty. It is less dusty than peat and almost equally absorbent. Although it is an excellent absorbent deep litter, yet it is not recommended for the north of West African countries. It breaks down easily into granules creating whitish dust on the walls. Poultry inhale the dust which creates chest congestion leading to fowl bronchitis.
3. STRAW AND CUT-STRAW: Whole straw will mat. The litter becomes damp and unpleasant if it is used as a starting material. Wheat straw is a little better than oat straw. Cut-straw can make a

useful litter. The length should not be more than (one and a half inches) 4 centimeter long.

4. SHAVINGS: Timber –shavings are very good and highly recommended. They are lighter than peat or saw dust. They do not tend to pad down so much. Their absorption capacity is good. They do not blow about easily. They are easily and cheaply obtainable. They can easily be removed and replaced. (Many people call this saw dust but it is not).
5. CHAFF: It is too light to be comfortable to birds. It scatters all over the place. It is too absorbent and it is not a really suitable material. Wool shoddy, shavings and oat hull are all the same not good.
6. COMBINATION: The following combinations can be used as a satisfactory base deep litter;
    i. Shavings and saw dust in equal quantities- saw dust as foundation.
    ii. Shavings and peat moss: 50- 50 . Use peat as foundation.
    iii. Shavings and cut straw: Shavings as foundation plus saw dust.
    iv. The middle (60,15,25) combination.

There are several other combinations. We should not forget to use sand when shavings or none of the above is available.

a. By far, the simplest method of starting the litter is to put into a depth of (six inches) 15 cm – wood shavings right away. This is called deep litter.
b. There is yet another method, you start with only (two inches) 5cm of litter, add to it at regular intervals, (say 2 weeks) as the dropping accumulate until the depth reaches 15cm for chicks and 23cm for pullets (6 in-8in).
c. The other practice is changing the litter at regular intervals. In school and colleges where poultry farm may be nearer to residential accommodation, the litter must be replaced every week. This will prevent odour and bad scent in the homes to the distaste of residents. This system is recommended only on the layer houses.
d. In the grower house, the litter is changed when the birds leave the house, but the litter must be dry.

e. Where the layer house is far away from human settlement, the litter can be allowed to build up for say six months.
f. In garages and backyards, the rooms must be cleaned every week for layer birds. The droppings contain ammonia which people do not like to smell. Ammonia is dangerous to health. So clean up more often. Ammonia can kill children, and even adults. The waste attracts flies into the nearby homes.
g. Not all people are interested in poultry and not many people like the smell that generates from your backyard. The smell affects neighbours. So keep it tidy.

CHAPTER 2: EGG PRODUCTION- THE MONEY SPINNER

There are many people in this country who do not fancy poultry as a business. For those people, I give few examples below:

Example 1: A colleague of mine has a teacher friend who reared 60 layers. These 60 layers produce 50 eggs per day- 350 eggs per week on average. 350 eggs are 29 dozen at $2 per dozen= $58 per week, $232 per month. He fed the chickens with maize and crumbs of bread and grass on free range.

Example 2: One Teacher reared 600 layers in two garages in his school residence. He lost 10 percent of the birds. So 540 survived. Of these 455 laid good eggs constantly. In one week, they laid 3,185 eggs approximately. These 3, 185 eggs are 265 dozens. They were sold at $2 per dozen=$530 per week. The 540 layers ate $5X 2X 7= $70 per week. The cost of electricity was $2 per week . So the total expenses were $72 per week (feed and electricity). Profit is sales- costs. Profit was $530- $72 =$458 per week For one month, the profit was $458 x 4weeks= $1,832.00.

The cost of labour, feed and electricity was $290 each month. The net profit was $1,542 per month= $15, 420 per annum. He later sold the 540 birds at $4 each= $2,160. The sum total of $15, 420 +$2, 160=$17,580 was made in one year. That is, if the eggs were sold at$2 per dozen. You can use this format and make your own calculations using the current price of egg per dozen. This is indeed a very profitable hobby, when you consider that the teacher is employed full time in the teaching profession at a salary of $4,800 per year. This gives him $400 per month compared with his hobby in chickens which gives him $1,832 per month. This work is done by one labourer for one year (10 months) continuous laying by the birds, the profit was (not chicken feed) $1,832 x 10= $18, 320 gross per annum. Net profit= $15,420. This teacher who uses my advice earns this to himself. No other hobby beats poultry keeping. You do agree with him. Don't you?

Example 3: A man went heavily into debt. He was allowed two years to pay back $250,000 but he had no means of doing so. Somebody mentioned him to me. When I wrote to help him at a fixed fee, he agreed but reluctantly. This was the outcome of our plans. He started with 1,500 layers. Each lay 900 eggs= 6,300 eggs , which was 525 dozens. This 525 dozens were sold at $200 per dozen= $10,500 per week.

Total profit for the first year was $42,000 x 10= $420,000. The expenses to be deducted were: Feeding costs=$100,800 per annum, Drugs= $10,000 per annum, Labourer and driver= $24,000 per annum. Total expenses were therefore, $134,800 per annum which when deducted from the income of $420,000 left him a net profit of $285,200 in the first year. He sold his birds at $40 each giving him $60,000 extra money. Total net profit= $385,200. This man never put his soul into the poultry business until now.

Example 4: A lecturer whom I met by accident, was fascinated buy the facts and figures in this manual, in manuscript form then. He rented four garages at $500 each per annum. He brought 100 day old chicks at 690 cents each= $6,900. At the end of the year, his profit was $35,480. The expenses deducted were; cost of day-old chicks= $690, cost of garages=$500, cost of feed=$2,500. Total expenses were= $3,690. Net profit was $35,480- $3,690 excluding $4,000 sales of 800 layers. The sum totalwas $35,790. Can any business beat the poultry business? I doubt it much.

NOTE: This lecturer was still teaching when he hit his jackpot. He planned to leave the service but I advised him not to until he had established a proper poultry farm. He could have done better initially had he bought the locally subsidized day-old chicks.

NOTE:

1. Poultry feed was subsidized at $50 per 25kg.
2. He asked me to plan for his gradual expansion. We constructed these buildings at a total cost of $18,000. The first house contained 100 layers, the second house contained the day-old chicks until they were on the point of laying, and the last contained 2,000 broilers. Broilers are marketed three times a year at 14 weeks old. This gives a total of 6000 broilers sold each year.
3. He sold 6,000 broilers at $40 each= $24,000 sales from the 100 layers at $50 per bird =$50,000 plus $3,800 egg sales. Total income from sales= $67,000. Deductions: Building costs=$18,000, Labourer, drugs and feed= $6000 . Net profit for the year= $43,000.

Let me remind you again that there is no business like the poultry business. You have only to accept this manual and follow it to the letter. Avoid talk and discussion and let the facts guide you through your present predicament. The examples are but a few of the many more that can be cited, but I do not want to bore you with figures. Egg production really is a money spinner.

NOTE: Remember: " Most people that are busy making a living do not make any money" Joe Karbo; Lazy man's way to riches.

CHAPTER 3: CARING FOR DAY-OLD CHICKS.

Some people may like to have simple incubators for practice. Incubators differ in operation. One thing is certain that though that the eggs must be in the incubator for 3 weeks, they should be turned from time to time.

The first two days after incubation are very critical in the life of chicks. After incubation and in the incubation room, day-old chicks should be out of the light completely. Keep them in a dark room or in cages, allowing enough fresh air to enter the enclosure. No food whatsoever should be given to them for the first two days after incubation. No artificial light is needed for the first 48 hours and no water should be given to them within the first 24 hours.

TREATMENT: Vaccinate against Newcastle diseases, chicken bronchitis and brooder pneumonia using either live or dead vaccines. Put a drop of the vaccine into the eyes of the day old chicks. This should be done right away from the moment they are hatched (see figure 6, table 7).

PREPARING TO RECEIVE THEM: After the first day, the day-old chicks are sent to the farm or are given to you, the farmer.

1. Prepare the Chicken house for the chicks to arrive. Disinfect it at least 24 hours before their arrival, and raise the temperature in the house to 95F.
2. The temperature is raised by closing all the windows and doors in the chicken house and leaving the light on for 24 hours.
3. Spread wood shavings, sand, hay, or dry wood chippings on the floor of the house.
4. Provide 15sq cm (6 inches) of room space per bird. To calculate this, measure the length and breath of the chicken house and multiply these figures obtained. Then multiply the product by 2 again.

(It is better to measure in feet). The new product is the number of day-old chicks required in that house. For example, a building (60ftx 30ft)=(180sq.ft). This gives a figure of 3600 day old chicks needed to fill that room.

5. Drinking space is at (3ft), 90cm intervals, ten 5-litre drinkers, 1 gallon (5 litres size) are sufficient for every 1,000 chicks from day old to 2 weeks.
6. At day-old, (1 gallon) 5 litres of water is needed for every 100 chicks and (3ft, 90cm) drinking space is just right in any room situated.
7. The drinking water is set out to at least a day (24 hours) before the chicks enter the house.

CHAPTER 4: BROODING ; DAY 1-5; THE FIRST WEEK OF LIFE FOR THE CHICK; DAY 1: THE DAY-OLD CHICKS HISTORY

Your day old chicks arrive on the farm today. Before you buy them, ask for their history, and remember to find out the following:

a. The parent hen's ability to lay more than 200 eggs.
b. The ability to lay large eggs.
c. The ability to lay continuously- persistency as they call it.
d. The ability to produce a strong egg shell.
e. Resistance to minor diseases, e.g. cold and heat.
f. The ability to eat less feed in proportion to eggs produced.

Do the following:

1. When they arrive, put newspaper on top of the wood shavings, sand, or wood chippings on the floor of the chicken house.

2. Throw the day-old chicks on the paper. Do not be gentle on them, as the procedure helps to cull the weak ones later.
3. Supply enough water in properly sealed troughs to prevent them from drowning.
4. Give 23 hours of light to the chicks at this stage, 12 hours day length plus 11 hours artificial light.
5. Today, (one gallon), 5 litres of water is needed for every 100 chicks.
6. Water must be available within (3ft), 90 cm of the birds at all times.
7. For the lighting, use 60 watt bulbs fixed into the ceiling at 30 cm intervals through out the entire house.
8. Fix half of the light with red bulbs (Davis red lamp). Any bulb of low density will be adequate. Red light should be 15cm from the floor.
9. Do not serve fresh water. It will give them pneumonia.

NOTE: Red bulbs control cannibalism and feather pecking. Only water is given to the chicks on the first day. No food. Note: 1ft= 30cm.

DAY 2: MILK AND GLUCOSE TREATMENT

1. Check for any sign of bacillary white diarrhoea (BWD) and diabetes. They are caused by vitamin deficiencies in the parent stock. It is a white sticky dropping covering the vent.
   a. These diseases are hereditary.
   b. They affect the newly hatched chicks during incubation.
2. All windows should remain shut.
3. The temperature should be 95 F.
4. There should be 23 hours of light.
5. If the old water gets finished, provide fresh water but do not wash the water troughs.

TREATMENT: To be used when the chicks have travelled for long distance (over 100km) to the farm and or where, the above mentioned diseases are to be stopped.

1. Give glucose (sugar) (4lbs), 2kgs in (1 gallon) 5 litres to prevent the diseases.
2. Supply (26 gallons), 130 ltres of drinking water to 1000 chicks daily.

3. Add 400 grains of full cream powdered milk, if available to the (26 gallons), 130 litres of water.

DAY 3: INTRODUCING THE FOOD TROUGHS

Today the chicks have to be provided with feeding troughs and the newspaper removed from the floor.

1. Provide fresh water, wash the water troughs for the first time, but if the milk is not finished, use the rest of the sugary water and the milk together.
2. Fill the food troughs 2/3 full to avoid waste.
3. Do not give fresh water and food at the same time. They should be provided on the same day, but not at the same time.
4. Remove all newspaper from on top of the wood shavings or sand.
5. There is still 23 hours of light needed.
6. The temperature is still at 95°F.

DAY 4: CULLING DAY

1. The water is changed three times and the chicks fed three times starting from today.
2. Three feeding methods are practiced.
   a. Three times a day on every week for every other day.
   b. Twice daily.
   c. Three times daily.
3. Experiments show that feeding three times daily is costly for the ordinary farmer. It may be fine in institutions where money is no problem and profit is not a goal. To feed the birds three times a day for every other day may be economical but is dangerous. You should use the twice daily method as that is economical and the birds eat every day.
4. The best time to serve the food is between 8.00 am- 9.00am and 4.00pm- 5.00pm.
5. The houses should be checked first thing in the morning to remove dead chicks.
6. From today, all chicks which show defects should be removed as the other birds easily catch the disease. This is called; calling the birds.

7. Culling must be through on the fourth day because it is a special day on the farm.
8. Culling means removing the defective chicks which show the following signs:
a. Small eyes.
b. Thrusted necks.
c. Chicks that keep falling over.
d. All weak looking chicks.
e. Chicks that are inactive.
f. Chicks with heavy or diseased abdomen.
g. Sleepy chicks.
h. Those with twisted toes and /or feet.
i. Chicks with blind or swollen eyes.
j. Those with twisted beaks.
9. Kill all defective chicks to avoid the spread of diseases.
10. Never mix, replace, or add new or strange chicks into a group. To avoid diseases, all birds must be of equal age.
11. Most of the windows should be opened to let in fresh air.
12. Reduce the number of chicks in the house by at least a 1/3 or divide up the group from the same room into two separate units and put them into different compartment.
13. Chicken pneumonia is brought in by overcrowding and cold weather below the room temperature ($60°$ F).
a. As soon as they recognize the familiar uniform of the farm worker, the chicks will come out of hiding.
b. If the chicks know the intruder, they come very close to welcome him or her.
c. They can only identify a person by his or her dress.
d. If they cannot recognize the appearance of the person, they intuitively sense danger, begin to quaver and shiver, and behave nervously.
e. Nervousness leads to many troubles in the farm, so avoid it.
f. Give glucose in the drinking water, if you notice signs of nervousness amongst them. Use one table spoon of glucose in 5 litres of water. Add milk at 1 teaspoonful to 5 litres of water.

NOTE:

1. It is difficult for the white race to recognize or differentiate between Africans and associate them with their country of origin.
2. It is impossible for Africans to identify whites with their country of origin barring language.
3. How on earth then, do you expect the poor chicken to differentiate between people- Musa from Amidu! John from Jane! Manager from Labourer!.
4. They do not understand your language but they do associate with different colours.

DAY 6: PREVENTION OF DISEASES

It is good that you provide anti-bacterial solutions for dis-infecting boots and shoes at the outside of the chicken house.

1. Use either Izal or Dettol in water.
2. Put the solution in a shallow trough immediately outside the door of the chicken house.
3. A shallow trough can be dug in the ground, cemented, left to dry and the liquid poured into it.
4. All farm workers should step in the disinfectant before they enter the chicken house.
5. It is economical to soak a jute sack in the liquid and leave it at the entrance. This stops people from getting their shoes and trouser wet.
6. The farm workers and visitors should step on the soaked sack before they go into the chicken house.
7. There is no need to change the solution, but extra liquid can be added to the sack.
8. Never place the disinfectant inside the house. The scent of it may be inhaled by the chicks.
9. Many chicks get nasal discharge caused by these disinfectants.
10. Stress it that everybody steps in the liquid only when they enter the house, but not when they leave.
11. Put a NO ENTRY sign on the doors of the house, so that no one goes in that way.
12. Give clean , fresh water each day. Wash the water containers once a day; first thing in the morning.

13. As soon as you finish feeding the chicks in the morning, clean and wash the food containers used a day previously.

NOTE: NEVER USE SOAP TO WASH FOOD OR WATER CONTAINERS.

Your chicks have survived the crucial seven days this first week. Congratulations! You are on the way to success, now let us look back and check up if we missed anything.

1. At the beginning of the 5th day, did you give glucose and milk powder as you did on the other day?
2. If yes, then repeat the same at the end of the week. i.e. today. Give 2kgs in (26 gallons) 130 litres of water. If no, then give 2kgs of glucose and powdered milk in (11 gallons) 55 litres of water.
3. Did you open the windows once more each day?
4. If yes, check the temperature in the room, it should be between 60 ° F- 80 ° F. That is a 75 ° F optimum.
5. Are you satisfied with the culling today, for it is dangerous to cull weak chicks among the flock. If yes, then look around and cull out any dull chicks.
6. Is there any disease affecting the chicks? If yes, look into their droppings. What are the signs?.
a. The most common disease is diarrhea. You can detect this by the white patches around the waste matter that the chicks discharge.
b. Another common disease is brooder pneumonia.

TREATMENT FOR THE ABOVE DISEASES

a. To cure disease (6a) above, use terramycin chick formula in water, ½ teaspoonful in one gallon of water (5 litres).
b. For diseases (6b), the outward signs are swollen eyelids; at a severe stage, the whole eyes closes up. Use the natural lime juice (from the lime tree) on the affected parts for three days (use once for protection and twice for cure). DO NOT USE IODINE as some inexperienced people may advice. Note: Many people mistake brooder pneumonia for fowl pox. Use iodine for fowl pox, but not for brooder pneumonia.

7. How many hours of light should the birds get now? They should receive only 12 hours of light: There is no more artificial light needed until they reach 15 weeks old.
8. Is the feed programme working? If the feed is enough, you will notice growth among the chicks. They must be healthy. They should run in the room and towards the feed and water for all these things are signs of growth. They should have developed feathers in their wings and tails. The males begin to show aggressive characteristics and are developing different feathers.
9. The food trough must be changed from a large square one to a narrow and restricted trough. The measurement of the new trough should be (2ft long by 131 wide and 61 long), 60 cm x 5cm x15 cm. One trough of this size should be used for 40 chicks.
10. Are you moving half of the birds to a different house? If yes, then do not change the wood shavings, clean or disinfect the room. If no, then move ½ of the chicks from the house. When the number is increased, stir up the wood shavings to provide a surface liter.
11. Open all windows to remove all feed troughs and drinking basins from the room whilst you stir up the wood shaving.
12. Sprinkle cold water on the wood shavings before you stir it up especially if the litter is dry and dusty.

NOTE:
1. Take all these precautions and let the birds start their second week with vigour.
2. Saw dust here refers to timber or wood shaving which has broken down into five granular material forming deep litter in the poultry house.

CHAPTER 5: WEEK 2-5, BROODING CONTINUES

WEEK 2: ROOM SIZE AND NUMBER OF CHICKS.

At the beginning of week 2, the chickens move on to a wider and more spacious room. Give each chick a space of one and half feet square (45 cm sq) in the room, for example, a room of (60 x 30) ft i.e. (1800 x 900 cm) now needs 1,200 chicks instead of 1,800 in 3, 600 as at a day old. Stir up the deep litter and turn it over to make it fresh. Where the litter is treated in this way, a disinfectant should be applied. If the wood shaving or deep litter was treated on day 5, then additional fresh wood shaving can be added on top of the old litter.

NOTE:

1. It is always dangerous to mix chickens from different environment.
2. Nobody should enter the house except the actual workers wearing their prescribed uniform, boots and caps.
3. The farm worker's uniforms must be kept in the farm premises unless they are to be washed.
4. The disinfectant outside the door of the chicken house should be removed occasionally.
5. When the birds are transferred to a larger room, the old room should be cleaned, swept and disinfected in that order.
6. Use either D.D.T , Izal or Dettol, or potassium permanganate solution to disinfect the room.
7. Leave the room for two weeks before a new batch of chicks move in.
8. During cleaning, the walls, windows, doors, ceiling and ventilation outlets should be cleaned as well.
9. After disinfection, all the windows, doors, and ventilators should be opened to allow good air circulation in the room.
10. Cleaning should be done in the proper order: (a) Removing saw dust (b) Sweeping the floor (c) Cleaning the walls and ceiling (d) Soaking and scrubbing, before washing the room.
11. Make sure all the feed troghs are thoroughly cleaned of old feed.
12. Do not use soap, chemicals or detergent in the feed troughs.

WEEK 3: TRACE ELEMENTS

1. Give complete starter rations to the chicks. Where such food is not available, add 20% protein to the normal maize flour for the next three weeks.
2. Add 1% of calcium to the food.
3. Add vitamins A, E and K in small quantities.

4. Add small quantities of trace elements to the food. Note: All the above elements can be found in cod liver oil.
5. For this week old chicks, the measurement of the ingredients is one tablespoonful per 25kg bag of feed.
6. Where vaccines are given in water, make sure that the water does not contain chlorine.
7. Be sure that all troughs are free from the smell and presence of disinfectant.
8. When an untreated water supply is used, add powdered evaporated milk to the water before serving it to the chicks.
9. Ordinary stream water should be purified as follows:
a. Use clean, white material to filter it.
b. Load stones, pebbles and pure stream sand into a perforated bucket.
c. Collect the purified water and add powdered evaporated milk.
d. Or boil the stream water and allow it to stand overnight before using it. Do this where powdered milk is not available.
e. Wells are also important. Dig a well and prepare it with clean, open and empty drums.
10. Water from wells need not be treated but instead treat the fowls with worm removal drugs every four weeks. Note: The 12 hours daylight, and 12 hours darkness should continue. Serve water three times a day, and feed twice a day.

WEEK 14: SKIMMED MILK FOR THE TREATMENT OF FOWL POX

Whenever water is to be added to any vaccine for the prevention of illness or disease, also a powdered skimmed milk at the rate of 100 g of skimmed milk to 40 litres of water. This solution is equivalent to 30 oz of milk per 100 litres of water. It is simpler to measure 1g of milk to 5 litres of water. Give the solution to the birds to drink instead. It is safer than injection.

INSTRUCTION:

1. Mix the powdered milk first, before adding the vaccine and not vice versa.
2. The milk protein neutralizes anything like chlorine or disinfectant present in the water.

3. The virus vaccine works longer when it is added to milk and proteins.

NOTE: Every 100 chicks drink 5 litres of water a day. That is, 1,000 chicks will need 50 litres of water a day. (One gallon equals five litres). Now your chicks have survived, one whole month with, or without, much trouble. Well done- you are on your way. Do you appreciate what you have achieved? Cast your mind back and recollect the day you made the bold decision to establish a poultry farm. Then visualize the actual day, you put this thinking into action and you can witness the dignity of labour.

4. Let the chicks remain in the larger room.
5. Let them drink the clean and treated water.
6. Check your medicine box to ensure that you have prepared against any outbreak of disease. Note: 1,000 ml= 1 liter.
7. Have terramycin soluble powder ready in the medicine box.
8. Prepare a bigger box to contain sections of different drugs, chemicals and powders.
9. Mark the box with different colours for easy identification.
10. Keep all medicines away from food, water, children and heat.

WEEK 5: DEBEAKING

Brooding ends this week and rearing starts this week. It is important to trim the beaks of all or some of the chicks this week.

1. Debeaking is to cut off 1 mm of the chicks beak.
2. Both upper and lower beaks are cut.
3. Remove two thirds of the beak (below the horn).
4. Be careful not to cut off the chicks tongue.
5. Debeaking is done at this stage because the horn of the beak becomes hard at the age of eight weeks.

NOTE: Deaking can bring about stress to the chicks, so help them by doing the following:

1. Include Vitamin K in the drinking water for 44 hours before debeaking.
2. Continue with this treatment for 24 hours after debeaking.

3. It is advisable not to debeak all the birds. Only the healthy ones should be debeaked.
4. Chicks with overlapping beaks should be examined and debeaked.
5. Debeaking should be done early in the morning or late in the evening.
6. Most poultry men prefer the evening to the morning as the birds will sleep and not use their sore beaks.

FEEDING:

1. As soon as the chickens are debeaked and for the next 3 days, fill the food troughs to the brim.
2. Help the chicks not to touch the bottom of the food trough with their sour beaks because it hurts them badly.
3. If this instruction is ignored, the birds may bleed from their beaks. The blood oozes into their mouths and they begin to like its taste.
4. When they grow accustomed to the taste of blood, they learn to peck their fellow weaker birds for more blood.
5. Blood tasting may lead them later to the drinking of their own eggs.
6. Blood tasting leads to cannibalism: Beware and be warned else you lose both birds and eggs.

CHAPTER 6; REARING: 6- 18 WEEKS

WEEK 6: THE GROWER PERIOD

There is no reason why the chicks cannot remain in the same house until the laying period, but you must provide plenty of ventilation, enough floor space and clean wood shaving from time to time. When it is impossible to get a larger house, the chicks can be moved from a brooding environment to a rearing house, and eventually to a layer- house.

1. There is not much difference physically between the chicks of last week and those of this week.
2. The most important difference between the brooding chicks and the rearing chick is the amount of medicine given.
3. The chicks still eat the same type of food. They need the same temperature and the same daylight length of 12 hours.

NOTE:

1. During the week, you must inject the chicks against Newcastle disease.
2. Call in a Veterinary Officer or Ministry of Agriculture Extension Officer , or report to the poultry production unit in your area for the drug.

3. Immediately after injection, protect the chicks against stress and strain by using any of the following medications.
a. Terramycin chick formula (See instruction on the packet).
b. Terramycin soluble powder in the drinking water.
4. Tylan drug in water protects the chicks against bronchitis.
5. Where no drugs are available, use sugar (glucose) in the drinking water, with or without powdered skimmed milk.
6. Start the chicks on grower feed next week.

WEEK 7: COCCIDIOSIS TREATMENT

1. Change the litter this week if the chicks were not move to a new rearing house.
2. If they are moved into a new house and a new environment, then make sure that they have enough milk and enough glucose.
3. The floor space should be (1ft . 6in) 45 cm square per bird.
4. The wire mesh in the new house should be much stronger than in the brooder house.
5. Wherever the chicks stay, they need treatment against coccidiosis this week.

NOTE: For coccidiosis treatment, use one of the following medicines.

1. Truthiodal , continuously in the feed for 2 weeks.
2. Amprolium powder in the drinking water for 10 days.
3. Zoalene in the drinking water for 2 weeks.
4. Metichlorphical in the drinking water for 2 weeks.
5. Metchlorphical in the feed for 4 weeks.

These medicines have their own manufacturer's instruction to which you must adhere to.

6. Before any medicine is given in the bird's drinking water, it is important to deprive the birds of drinking water for at least 12 hours in tropical areas and 24 hours in temperate areas.
7. Do not provide the same drug in water and food , for the same birds on the same farm , at the same time.
8. Try to avoid overdose of medicines.

9. Record all medicines given to the birds, when it was given, which house, what age group, where the medicine was purchased, and its price, all must be recorded.
10. Record the facts in a notebook and read it over from time to time, at least once a month.

WEEK 8: SICK BAY TREATMENTS

Your chicks are two months old this week. You must again cull the sick and treat them where possible. Make out a spacious room where the sick birds are kept, treated, experimented on and tried with new drugs. Call the room "Sick Bay".

1. It is not possible to isolate each and every sick bird or even to group different diseases together.
2. Mix all the sick birds in one big room.
3. Inspect the sick bay daily to see the effect of the improvement. Record the diseases which were cured first in the sick bay and the date they left; if they ever leave. Record the time the sick birds entered the sick bay and the date they leave if they ever leave.
4. Record which drug or medicine cured which disease and for how long.
5. Always feed the healthy birds first. Feed them, serve them with water and finish the work there before you visit the sick bay.
6. Serve the sick bay birds with feed and water. Group them according to their age.
7. It is convenient and economical that a special worker looks after the sick bay.

FOR THE HEALTHY BIRDS.

1. Vaccinate all of them against fowl pox for the first time this week. It will be too late to prevent it, if you do not vaccinate them.
2. Inspect daily and cull out the weaker birds.
3. Weigh the chicks, five at a time, and then find the average weight.

For example, 5 birds weigh 3kg, 3kg, 2kg, 2kg and 2kg. Total weight adds up to 12kg.

4. Divide the total weight by the number of birds= 12/5 = Average weight per bird.
5. Where the weight is less, add more protein to the feed.
6. Where the weight is more, reduce the food intake.

Note: 1kg= 1000g =2lb.

WEEK 9: RESTING WEEK FOR HYGIENE

1. Give ordinary clean or treated water to the birds 3 times a day.
2. Feed twice a day as usual.
3. Examine the effect of the feeding programme twice a day.
4. Find out how best you can improve on the system.
5. Where you find the weight to be of normal average, continue with the feeding programme.
6. If there are problems with the programme, then try to improve it.
7. You may improve the feeding system by increasing the frequency of feeds to 3 times a day at 8am, 4pm and 5pm.
8. You may choose to retain the twice daily feeding system with some addition or modification- adding protein as in the other week.
9. Add more wood shavings on top of the old litter or stir up the old litter.
10. Where the weather is of the North African type- very dry and dusty, sprinkle water on the litter every other week.
11. Dusty litter causes lung congestion among the birds.
12. Lung congestion causes bronchitis and difficult breathing.
13. Bronchitis is a deadly disease among poultry especially at this stage.
14. Bronchitis is also cause by visitors and farm workers smoking cigarettes in the chicken house. There should be a " No smoking" sign in the house and on the farm.
15. In both cases, the birds inhale the smoking and/or the dusty particles which block their wind pipes.
16. Bronchitis is the cause of about 90% of deaths among the sick birds.
17. Bronchitis is an infectious disease which spreads in the air and trough feed and drinking water. Note: Avoid bronchitis by all means and at all costs.

Table 1 ; Figure 1: Feed consumption rate

GROWERS		LAYERS	
AGE IN WEEKS	FEED PER BIRD PER DAY IN GRAMS	AGE IN WEEKS	FEED PER BIRD PER DAY IN GRAMS
0-8	54	19	88
9	54	20	91
10	56	21	96
11	60	22	104
12	64	23	108
13	68	24	119
14	72	25	111
15	75	26	111
16	78	27	111
17	81	28	112
18	85	29	112
19	90	30	112
20	93	31	103
21	97	33	111
22	100	33	113
23	123	34	112
24	140	35-40	113
25	149	41-50	112
26	151	51-60	111
27	159	61-74	108

NOTE: Antibiotics stimulate growth in 10 weeks. The birds are still on a 12 hours day length programme.

WEEK 11: CLEANLINESS

Check for general cleanliness and hygiene in the buildings. Among the birds and with anything which needs to be cleaned or washed.

1. Clean all cobwebs on the window stalls on the ceiling, at the four corners of the houses and between the wire mesh.
2. List all boxes on which water and feed troughs stand.
3. Beware of mice and cockroaches which might hide under such water soaked boxes.
4. Many diseases on the farm originate from feed and after being contaminated with mice faeces, mice urine and cockroaches droppings.
5. Destroy such mice and cockroaches found hiding under the boxes. Kill them.
6. Seek and destroy rats around the area. Rats like mice contaminate feed and water. They come to enjoy themselves and help themselves to the chicken feed at night.
7. By eating the food, they put germs into the feed.
8. The feed becomes foul and immediately the hens picks a crumb which had fallen down, it gets sick and may die as a result.
9. Plagues might set in among the poultry. If more of such rats are allowed in unchecked.
10. Treat termites like you treat mice and cockroaches, though termites do not cause diseases. They would rather eat the feeding troughs and almost anything else except iron and stone.

Note: Seal off all holes to stop snakes, mice and rats entering the house.

WEEK 12: TREATMENT OF COLDS

Revaccinate against Newcastle disease and fowl pox.

1. In week 12, diseases are many but the most outstanding of the lot is coccidiosis.
2. Watch out for the following diseases as well if the birds were not vaccinated against them previously.
3. This is the age of trouble. So beware and be warned.

Note: In the poultry industry, prevention is preferred to cure of anxiety, uncertainty and eventual bad luck (If you believe in luck, that is).

1. Provide Amprolium for prevention and cure of bronchitis for the first 3 days.
2. Amprolium is one of the best medicines for coccidiosis diseases.
3. After this treatment, give clear drinking water on the 4th day as well.
4. Two days after the treatment with Amprolium, start using cod liver oil in the feed.

MEASUREMENT

1. Give one tablespoonful of cod liver oil in a bag (25kg) of feed for the rest of the week. (4 days).
2. Where bronchitis and/or Marek's disease rather than coccidiosis is the problem, then give terramycin.

WEEK 13: CHANGING FEEDING HABITS

Continue with your normal feed programme, that is, twice for feeding and 3 times for water.

1. This week, your chicks have entered into a new phase. They are new teenagers, and they show different behavior and aggressive attitude towards one another.
2. The troubles you will encounter are those of teenage show-offs. Like human beings, the teenage girls show female characteristics.
3. They go out early and come home late. They also eat more to grow and build up tissue.
4. Pullets form round female bodies with short feathers, short legs, small dames and small wattles.

5. Male cockerels show longer legs, well developed dames and wattles and well protruding tail feathers.
6. Like teenagers, they go off their food and lose appetite in the presence of the opposite sex.
7. You can explore and use this poultry psychology to your advantage. On their own, they eat very much.
8. Introduce a few cockerels among the pullets.
9. The best combination is 10 cockerels to 100 pullets.
10. This ratio will stop the males fighting for possession of the "girls".
11. The presence of the opposite sex will put them on a diet to your advantage.
12. The males will run after the females round the house. Both birds will show enthusiasm in the hide and seek game all the time.
13. Males will show aggression and vigour in the game.

Note: Provide more carbohydrate feed. Add more cassava flour to a total quantity of 65% of cassava or maize. Give plenty of water this week but there should be no change in the light programme. Fill the feed trough only to ¾ full to avoid waste.

WEEK 14: BUILDING WEIGHT

Provide something for them to get weight because they lose weight through running around so much in week 13.

1. Provide grit as the only feed for the whole of this week.
2. The grit can be in the form of limestone, shale, or common river sand.
3. Make your own grit feed with sand from river beds or sited area sand after heavy rains.
4. Collect the sand, sieve the pebbles out and retain the finest, shiny white or brown sand. Wash the sand thoroughly. Dry it, pack in sacks and take them to the farm. Give quantities of the sand to the birds to eat. Never mix sand with food as this is dangerous. Some yellowish brown sand can be collected from gallous or gutters after heavy rains. Wash this with ordinary water before use. Do not wash with soap or any detergent.
5. The most common diseases in week 14 are: Liver leucosis and bronchitis. Once again, use Amprolium (Amprol for short). In places where Amprol is

not available, use one or any of the following: (a) Suphanidine (b) Suphaquinozadine (c) Nitrofurosine.

NOTE: The sand helps to reduce the intake of food. The sand makes them heavy so as to avoid excessive light weight. Remember that if your poultry are broilers then this is the week to sell them. Broilers only stay on the farm for 14 weeks, then they are sold to the public as table birds. The practice is a good one. Follow it and save money.

WEEK 15 : FOWL POX

Do not stop abruptly to introduce proper feed. The withdrawal of sand feed must be gradual. Remember not to mix sand in the feed.

1. This week, provide sand side by side with the grower feed.
2. The feed and sand are provided separately in different feeding troughs.
3. Do not change the size, shape, or colour of the feed troughs.
4. Feed should be in the usual and accustomed troughs.
5. Put the sand in bigger (square) trays.
6. Use the one week old chicken troughs as sand trays.
7. The sand is now served to pullets about to be transferred into the layer house in a few weeks' time.

NOTE: Treat fowl pox again this week. Better still prevent any outbreak of disease.

1. One day in a week, provide vitamin A medicine for the prevention of food pox.
2. The birds have reached a stage where the internal organs are changing and developing to produce the hormones for egg production. Among the higher animals, it is called puberty. Puberty creates heat troubles and headache among all animals and birds. Supply antibiotics for fowl pox, infectious laryngotrochitis and infectious bronchitis, fowl typhoid, fowl pox, Leucosis complex, Newcastle diseases, Avian manocytosis and Marek's disease. All can manifest themselves from this week onwards.

3. The antibiotics used for the prevention of these diseases are (a) Euraviste (b) Floxaid (c) Terramycin poultry formular. For prevention, use one packet for 100 litres (22 gallons) of water for 5 days.

WEEK 16: FEEDING; ALTERNATIVE METHODS.

Stop feeding the pullets with sand.

1. Remove the sand trays but leave the food troughs.
2. Do not change the feeding pattern which is twice daily.
3. Continue with grower mash.
4. Nothing is more wasteful than over-feeding the pullets.
5. Overfed pullets became extra heavy at their abdomen.
6. The pullets cannot convert the extra feed into eggs at this age of 16 weeks.
7. Extra feed is therefore converted to fat.
8. Too much fat can block the sac passage or reduce its elasticity, thereby preventing easy passage of eggs in the future.
9. Too much fat generates heat inside the abdomen.
10. Too much heat can destroy the egg sac and the eggs inside the hen.
11. Nothing will stop you from feeding the pullets 3 times a day, but if you do, make sure that they need the food.
12. Another alternative for feeding the pullets is three times a day on every other day. MEANING: You feed three times today, you miss tomorrow and feed 3 times again the day after tomorrow.
13. Missing a day is cumbersome and dangerous.
14. So stick to the twice daily feeding for everyday.
15. You have to safeguard the health of the pullets.

NOTE: Use piperazine compounds to treat worms this week. You save much money by decreasing the amount of money spent on food daily. Now check how much you have spent on food alone. Count the number of sacks recorded in your purchasing book and multiply the number by the cost per bag, whatever you arrive at represents the cost of twice feeding daily. Add half of the cost to the figure arrived at for 3 times feeding daily.

EXAMPLES: Twice feeding 3 days a day for 7 days= 21 days.

21 bags at $90 each = $1,890. There are 112 bags more making 4,124 bags a day for 7 days= 31, 812 bags. 31,812 bags of $90 each =$92, 830.50k. But every 600 birds twice feeding saves you $940 per week ($2880.50- $1890= $940.50). This saves $370 on feeding and saves money. Np further vaccination after week 16.

WEEK 17: GREEN LEAVES IN THE FEED (TRACE ELEMENTS).

Poultry feed which has been stored up over one month has lost its flavour.

1. Add fish liver oil, cod liver oil , or green leaves to the pullet ration this week.
2. Fish liver oil, cod liver oil and green leaves all contain trace elements and they are rich in vitamin A.
3. Poultry need vitamins A, K and E but no more A is needed.
4. Cod liver oil that has been kept in a store for up to 3 months loses its vitamin A content.
5. You will be better off to supply green leaves to the birds.
6. It is easier to cut your lawn and give the grass to the birds.
7. Go to various schools and ask to cut their football pitch free of charge. The school authorities will welcome your offer and the pupils will help you willingly.
8. Chop the grass into little bits before you give it to the birds.
9. Experiments have proved that they can live on grass alone as feed.
10. Always give the weed raw and fresh to the birds. You can grind the grass and make pellets out of it.
11. Dry the pellets (in the sun) where possible.
12. Let the pellets cool down for 24 hours before giving them to the birds.
13. Any edible leaves could be served to poultry.
14. Leaves such as cocoyam leaves, cassava leaves, banana leaves or alfalfa can be used.
15. All local edible leaves are good. Use them to reduce feed cost.
16. Do not boil the leaves.
17. Do not mix leaves with the feed . Serve leaves separately before or after the main feed.
18. Green leaves help to produce better golden yolk in the eggs.
19. Do not heap the leaves. If they are mashed, spread them to dry.

NOTE : The birds can be choked if they swallow lots of leaves at once. The 12 hours day length programme continues this week. A new programme starts next two weeks.

WEEK 18: AIM AT LIVE WEIGHT OF THE BIRDS.

1. The new light programme starts at the end of the week.
2. Until now, the birds have been receiving only 12 hours of daylight which contributes to feed consumption by the poultry.
3. The method stopped them from eating all night.
4. At the end of this week, catch 5 pullets and weigh them.
5. Select the birds at a random sample- do not be selective on the big birds only.
6. Bind the legs of each bird together and weigh them on a spring balance.
7. At this stage, the range of the body live weight must be between 1.45 and 1.55 kgs. The average weight must be about 1.50kgs.
8. Finish weighing more of them by the end of this week.
9. It is advisable to box up all the pullets you weighed to avoid weighing wrong group of birds.
10. Prepare the layer house before they are sent in.
11. Send in layer cages a day or two before the chicken arrive.
12. Prepare waste matter platform covered with (2/3 in) 2 cm wire mesh.
13. The platform will serve as the waste pit for all the birds.
14. The layer-cages should be filled with something soft. Saw dust, small seeds, sand or the dead bark of a banana plant is well softened.
15. The layer cases entrance should face the wall.
16. Cages should be shut at night but open during the day so as to prevent the birds using the cages as sleeping places.

NOTE: Mix the pullets with cockerels at a ratio of 100 pullets to 10 cockrels or 10 to 1 of the eggs needed for incubation.

CHAPTER 7: NEW LIGHT PROGRAMME BEGINS

WEEK 19: THREE PROGRAMMES IN ONE WEEK.

Three programmes are to be carried out today. Lighting, catching the pullets and transporting them from the grower house to the layer house. All are heavy duties. Use blue light bulbs when you are catching the bird, because they are docile in light. This job must be done at night.

1. The pullets are still teenagers and they are very strong and therefore difficult to catch.
2. Use a large net to surround small groups at a time. Catch those first and inject them with an anti-stress and strain drug. (Consult your veterinary officer for the drugs).
3. Put them at least 2 weeks before the 21st week.
4. Transport them under darkness; do not allow the birds to notice their new environment.
5. Weigh the same birds again.
6. Release them all after you have weighed them.

LIGHT PROGRAMME.

The new light programme for layers starts this week.

1. Add 30 minutes to the length of daylight, which now becomes 12 ½ hours.
2. Put on the artificial light from 6pm until 6:30 pm everyday throughout the week.

3. After 6:30 pm, the pullets go back to stay in total darkness until the next day.
4. After this week, provide only 15 minutes of extra light every day.
5. Provide layer nests and provide a pit.
6. Do not change the pattern or colour of the feeding and water containers.
7. Almost all the pullets will lose as much as (1lb to 2lb), 500g to 1000g weight.
8. To prevent SOLINSTER STRESS, put medicine in the drinking water.
9. Give the medicine, first thing in the morning after their arrival.
10. Debeak again pullets which were not properly debeaked before and those whose beaks have grown again. (See week 5).
11. Light out at 6:30pm, give exactly 12 ½ hours light throughout week 9.
12. Repeat (25kg) of layer mash.

Table 2: Skillful use of artificial light

Pullets	Morning (a.m)	Morning (a.m)	Evening (p.m)	Evening (p.m)
Weeks old	From	To	From	To
19	5.30	6	6	6.30
20	5.15	6	6	6.45
21	5.00	6	6	7.00
22	4.45	6	6	7.15
23	4.30	6	6	7.30
24	4.15	6	6	7.45
25	4.00	6	6	8.00
26	3.45	6	6	8.15
27	3.30	6	6	8.30
28	3.15	6	6	8.45
29	3.00	6	6	9.00
30	2.45	6	6	9.15
31	2.30	6	6	9.30
32	2.15	6	6	9.45
33	2.00	6	6	10.00
34	1.45	6	6	10.15
35	1.30	6	6	10.30
36	1.15	6	6	10.45
37-40	1.00	6	6	11.0

NOTE: Use the light either in the morning or in the evening. 1000g=1lb=1kg.

WEEK 20: MINERALS IN THE FEED

Do not give the pullets the complete layer mash yet. Wait until 5% of the birds start laying. 5% means 50 eggs laid among 1000 pullets, or 5 eggs laid among 100 pullets. The light programme this week is lights out at 6.45pm.

1. After 5% of the pullets have laid, then give layer mash.
2. Give more calcium in the feed.
3. The more calcium in the feed, the stronger the egg shell.
4. The calcium content in the feed should be 1%.

This 1% means 1kg of calcium in one bag (25kg) of layer mash.

5. Continue the calcium intake throughout all of week 20.
6. Apart from calcium, provide more protein in the feed.
7. Add one table spoonful of cod liver oil into one bag (25kgs) of layer feed.
8. Treat for BWD diseases for 3 days with Amprol powder in the drinking water.
9. Administer drugs in clean water (see day2).

NOTE: This week, the body weight should be 1.55- 1.65kg (3.4- 3.6lb).

WEEK 21: AIMING FOR EARLY MATURITY

Early matured pullets will show signs of laying before they are 6 months of age. Three things emerge this week. So note:

1. For those transferred into the deep litter house, wood shavings must be 6in (15cm) deep to prevent the eggs from cracking. When only plentiful commercial eggs are needed, no cocks should be among the hens.
2. If the eggs are needed for incubation, then follow these instructions:

For every 10 hens, add one cock, for every 100 hens add one cock, for every 1000 hens add 100 cocks. This is a 10 to 1 ratio as already mentioned. Both the hens and cocks should be from different parents which have these identical qualities.

a. Persistency- Ability to lay everyday.
b. Egg number beyond 240 per season.
c. Egg weight- not below par.
d. Egg quality- good shell.
e. Hatchability of eggs- able to hatch when put in an incubator. When the above mentioned quality are satisfied, then you mate the cocks and the hen.

WARNING: Never mate hens and cocks from the same parents. Unrelated birds produce better and more eggs. They produce better offsprings that are healthy and strong, and have bigger layer muscles. That is why, it is profitable to mate locals with foreign breeds.

3. For pullets transferred into battery cages, be sure to place them carefully and gently inside the cages. The most economical and stress free type are dual

cages, where two birds are placed in one cage. The disadvantage is that you cannot know which birds are not laying. So choose single cage birds and replace them at will. Though single cages are dearer and they occupy more space.

NOTE: The light programme is new artificial light from 6pm to 7pm making 13 hours of light.

WEEK 22: BURY THE DEAD.......HYGIENE

1. Inspect the hens and cull (take away) the sick, deferred cases and the outcasts. The light programme for week 22 is from 6pm to 7.15 pm (13 hours total). One or two hens would have laid by now. They are the early matured pullets.
2. Give the birds half grower and half layer feed. They still eat twice a day but water is given 3 times a day.
3. Continue with clean water unless there is an outbreak of a disease.
4. Inspect the locks and remove the dead birds, if any. Bury dead birds deep in the soil. Do not leave them on rubbish heaps.
5. Dead birds spread disease greater than live ones, so be warned.

WEEK 23: PRODUCTION RATIO.

1. By now a small number of the early matured birds have laid their first eggs. Congratulations! You are in business.
2. If you have 50 eggs among 1000 hens then that is sufficient for the birds to go on full layer mash for smaller poultry farms. 10 eggs among 100 birds are required before going on to layer mash. The artificial light needed in the week is from 6 pm to 7.30 pm.
3. Cure with an antibiotic drug for the first 3 days! Use Terramycin poultry formular in water. For birds in deep litter, add a little fresh wood shavings on top of the old. \
4. Keep everything clean. Wash troughs every morning and dry them in the sun.

CHAPTER 8: THE LAYING PERIOD: WEEK 24 TO WEEK 72.

WEEK 24: HOUSING THE PULLETS

This is the production week. The majority of the young hen (pullets) will lay their first eggs ever this week, even the late developers. Continue with 2 feeds and 3 water drinking times a day. Wash the feed and water troughs once every morning. Soak the trough together in a big concrete bunker specially constructed outside the poultry house. Soak the troughs a day before. The soaking makes all the old caked feeds to remove. Use hard, bristle brush for the job. For battery cages, bring all feed containers down.

Once a week, scrub them clean. Allow them to dry and set them back the same day. Water tubes or bars should never be moved. Use a small brush to clean the water contained by collecting the dirty water at one end of the containers. The light is from 6pm to 7.45 pm. The protein level this week is 18 g.

WEEK 25: NUTRIENT LEVEL

Be sure to adjust nutrient levels under severe (cold or tropical heat) conditions. Management of conditions or changes in farm hands can greatly affect the total feed intake. This you must watch and record.

Try to stimulate the feed intake or increased protein level in the feed. It costs to increase the protein intake than to increase feeding. To supplement your protein addition, add cod liver oil, extra fish meal or soya bean meal. Any of these three will go a long way to make a balanced feed. Light is from 6pm – 8pm.

WEEK 23: PROTEIN FOODS

Provide one phase feeding method at this period of laying. At least 18 gms of good protein must be eaten per hen per day. This helps them to lay, good shelled and good size eggs as well as giving peak and quality eggs production. Artificial light should be given from 6pm to 8:15 pm. Provide 1 to 3kg calcium in the feed of 25kg per bag.

CHAPTER 9 : BROODING 100 CHICKS OR MORE FOR EGGS.

1. Clean , wash and thoroughly disinfect the chicken house and equipment THREE WEEKS before the chicks arrive. Mop pools of water and make sure walls and floors are perfectly dry. Build a concrete bunker (90:90:60)cm outside the house.
2. Spread sand or shavings at 1 bag (25kg feed bag) per 9 square yard), 90 sq. cm or use (per 100 sq. feet) 3,000 sq.cm . This will give (after spreading) a depth of 15cm (6 inches) but 7 ½ cm after 4 days when pressed by the chicks running on it.
3. Two days before the chicks arrive, close up air and fan vents and close all windows.
4. Set the electric bulbs at 300 cm (10ft) apart.
5. Also set the infra red bulbs at 8 cm above the floor under the boxes. Use this for brooders.
6. Provide boxes in the room; 1 box for every 250 chicks.
7. Place a 60 cm high surround of cardboard or hardboard about 912 ft or 360 cm. Leave it on its own in the tropics.
8. Place 10 tabular feeders evenly firmly. Each one circular surrounded and pressed down firmly by each one in the litter.
9. Place (10 gallons) , 50 litre troughs of water in the circle close to the center.
10. If automatic drinkers are provided, they should be switched on , one day after the chicks have arrived; but test them before hand.

11. On the remaining spaces, spread newspaper.
12. On the second day in the house, spread chick mash on the paper for the chicks to eat. This will be their 3rd day from incubation.
13. Switch on lights 48 hours before the chicks arrive.
14. Hang a maximum and minimum thermometer in the house to read the temperatures everyday.
15. When the heat is over 100 °F, open some windows to let some air in. When the heat is below 60 °F, close the windows to raise the temperature.
16. When the chicks arrive, cull out the weak ones immediately. Never open the boxes or release the chicks below a temperature of 60 °F.
17. Once a chick is warm, it will eat and drink. The rest is daily observation and reasoning.
18. Clean the drinkers and refill them daily.
19. On the 4th day, expand the surrounds. (the enclosure of cardboards).
20. Reduce the temperature slowly by opening one window at a time.
21. Remove newspapers spread on the wood shavings after 30 days. Never fill feeders more than 2/3 full.
22. One percent of the chicks are bound to die. The good brooding and rearing methods laid down in this manual mean that, at least 95% of those you have paid for as day old chicks will be fit to go into the laying house. You may lose another 1% during the laying period for unforeseen circumstances.
23. NUTRITION DEFECTS: For nutrition defects, add cod liver oil to the feed at the rate of 2 tablespoonful to 25kg of feed.
24. DISEASES: Check the appearance of the waste matter. Look for signs of coccidiosis which is signified by blood stained water.
25. Provide dry litter and give Amprolium. Amprolium and all Amprol drugs are effective.
26. Some cockrels have drugs like pullets, so be observant and cull (remove) them from among the hens. Give them antibiotic drud, Terramycin every two weeks to avoid any unexpected disease coming at production time.
27. TEMPERATURE: High temperature adversely affect egg shell quality. Egg shell quality naturally declines with age of the flock. Lighting time is from 6pm to 9.45 pm.

WEEK 27: SPECIAL MONTHS.

Concentrate your efforts to improve the egg shell quality in hot weather. Damage is caused in June, July and August in temperate and mountanous countries: December and January in the forest zones ; (rainfall 150- 360 cm); February, March and April in semi desert regions (rainfall 90-110 cm); December, January and February in most tropical countries and savanna belt areas where rainfall is between 110 cm and 150 cm. Check which months apply to your state /region and farm from the above list.

Identify the zone in which you are working and prepare against possible damage to the eggs in each seasons. Consult the atlas map if you are not sure or ask a friend. Lighting is from 6.00pm to 12.00pm. Continue with clean water and feeding programmes.

WEEK 28: SODIUM BICARBONATE IN THE FEED

Shell quality is naturally improved in the tropical world by reducing the quantity of salt in the feed to only 2%. Then add ¼ lb (12 ½ g). For whole week, feed the entire flock with oxytotetracycline- 100 per ton of feed. This is only in acute cases where every other treatment has failed. The egg shell will improve in no time, but only for a short period enough for small poultry farms. Lighting time is from 6pm t0 10: 15 pm.

WEEK 29: COMMERCIAL FARMS USE OYSTER SHELL

You have treated the chickens which were laying poor quality eggs. Now for large commercial farms, use 2/3 lb, 37 ½ g of oyster shell and 1/3 lb , 25 g limestone per bag of feed. Grind them together or separately and continue this for the rest of the production period. Limestone can be obtained from any cement factory. Terrazzo manufacturers can provide you with oyster shell or coiled snail shells. Mash them and grind them and your calcium feed is complete. Do not try anything expensive. Always achieve maximum efficiency at minimum cost. Lighting time is 6pm to 10.30 pm.

WEEK 30: CHECK PERFORMANCE LEVEL

This week, your hens are 9 months old. Many have been laying for 3 months and they have reached excellent production. They have been developed for top performance. They can reach their production maximum in the cage, on litter, or on free range yards, if the preceding management, nutitional recommendation and drug programmes were followed week by week. They are guaranteed to produce the maximum number of eggs with the highest profit margin. You will receive top quality eggs per hen- up to 74 weeks of age. Change the litter this week. Do not disinfect, only clean and put fresh wood shavings in. Collect the eggs 3 times a day immediately after feeding time. Lighting time is 6pm to 10.45 pm.

WEEK 31: PEAK PERIODS

Week 31 is the beginning of the second quarter of the laying period. Hens start during laying eggs during week 24 and they stop laying during week 74. This means that they lay continuously for 50 weeks (11 ½ months), and then 2 months' rest.

Lighting time is from 6pm to 11pm and they should continue every day until week 72. This gives the maximum 17 hours of light (12 hours daylight plus 5 hours of artificial light). From this week onwards, everything is constant. The rest is by observation and repetition of feeding and drugs. After 6 months of production, increase the calcium content of the feed.

WEEK 32: FEED NEEDS VITAMINS

Both deep litter and battery cage layers require less concentrated mash. Animal protein content of 15 ½ % in the mash is enough. Add vitamins A and B3 by including 1 ½ % pints of cod liver oil per cwt (112lbs) of mash or 15kg or 2 bags of feed. An alternative method of supplying these vitamins is the inclusion of 5% grass meal in the ration, Vitamin B complex and many other nutrients. Give ordinary clean water and 17 hours of light is enough.

WEEK 33: FEED NEEDS LIME

A further 1% of ground limestone should be supplied. Calcium should be added to the ration for heavier birds. Add salt at the rate of ½ % and 4 oz of magnesium sulphate if available. Give water 3 times and feed twice a day. Light out at 11pm.

WEEK 34: MORE CARBOHYDRATE AND FLINT

Carbohydrate feed in the ration should be 60% while cereals if added should not be more than 10%. Add flint to aid digestion. It should be given separately and not be added to the feed. A good source of carbohydrate food is tapioca or cassava flour. Give Terramycin antibiotic in the water this week.

WEEK 35: FEED LESS GRAIN BUT MORE PROTEIN

Check on egg production. Inadequate feeding is the chief cause of poor egg production, and the most common mistake is feeding on excessive proportion of green. Where the grain intake exceeds the amount of protein, the effect of the vitamins and minerals is lessened and egg production is lowered. Give cod liver oil to raise protein level in the feed.

WEEK 36: ADD MILK IN THE FEED

Where milk is available in either powdered or liquid form, give 5 litres (one gallon) for every 20 layers. The milk will balance the cereal and also substitute for animal protein, minerals and vitamins – except A and B3. Milk should be given to the brooding flock and growing chickens as well as the layers. Light out at 11 pm.

WEEK 37: CHECK PROFITS AND RECORD

Check your records. Look through them thoroughly and find out how many bags of feed the layers and other hen eat, as well as how many eggs are laid. Contact your sources of feed supply and buy the feed in bulk to get discount prices. Almost (85%) of the layers lay eggs now, so contact women and firms who make cakes to sell all your broken eggs to them. If more eggs are broken, give Minovet again in the feed. Tea spoon –full of Minovet in 1 bag (25kgs) of feed will reduce cracking within 3 days and stop it in 5 days. You should mix Minovet thoroughly in the feed before giving it to the birds.

WEEK 38: MORE MARKET OUTLETS

The layers have now laid continuously for 20 weeks and they are in peak form. Make contact with schools, hospitals, colleges, universities, hotels and supermarkets for quick sales and rapid turnover. Be flexible in your approach and give discounts to these institutions.

WEEK 39: CHANNELS OF DISTRIBUTION

Record keeping continues. Do you sell your empty feed bags? Do not give them away but sell them to reduce feed costs. Continue with record keeping and be strict with employees more now than ever before. If you do not warn them, you will encourage them to drink the eggs raw and give them away to relatives. They think of the production but not the cost, and they will demand payment externally. To be strict is to be successful. So be strict.

WEEK 40: NO VISITORS AND NO SMOKING

Avoid visitors at all costs. Visitors , no matter their social status, should never be allowed to enter the laying house but should watch the layers through the windows. Smoking is strictly forbidden anywhere near the layers and prohibited in all the houses. Be more strict on the relative of workers and do not allow them to deceive the labourers and farm workers.

WEEK 41: ACCOUNTS

Record keeping is essential in order to reduce costs. Records give accurate picture of spending , food consumption, egg production and feed costs. Keep useful accounts of laying birds, egg and feed consumption, medication, labour costs and eggs given to very important persons (VIPs).

WEEK 42-49: IMPORT EXPORT, SALESMEN OR AGENTS.

Order for our import export operations manual to enable you practice

importation and exportation of products. Employ salesmen and other farm workers to spread the selling far and wide. Try to export your poultry products and expertise to other countries, if you need foreign money. You can appoint an agent who will charge only a commission. He/she will find you the outlets where you can sell direct. Your salesmen can cover your own country. Never appoint salesmen abroad without studying the principles of exporting in our step by step guide to import export business training manual to avoid business mistakes that leads to loss of effort, energy, time and money. Contact us for further information on how to import or export poultry products efficiently and profitably.

WEEK 50: ONWARD SURVEYING OF THE MARKET

Think about starting broilers in the empty rooms. Work out the demand for meat in your area and in your country. Work out how the broilers will be sold and at what price. Sell live birds rather than prepared ones. Most people buy the bird from outward appearance. Some people may like to weigh them.

Keep in mind that yellow footed birds sell better in the tropics and pale footed birds sell well in temperate regions. The body weights this week should be between 1.82 – 2.02 kg (4lb- 4.41 lb). The last weighing is on week 72. The body weight then should be 1.900- 2.10 kg (4.2- 4.6 lb)

CHAPTER 10: BROODING 1000 CHICKS OR MORE FOR EGGS

1. Clean, wash and thoroughly disinfect the chicken house and equipment THREE WEEKS before the chicks arrive. Mop pools of water and make sure walls and floors are properly dry.
2. Spread sand or shavings at 1 bag (25kg feed bag) per (square yard), 90 sq. cm or use 1 ton (per 100 square feet) 300 sq cm. This will give (after spreading) a depth of 15cm, (6 inches) but 7 ½ cm after 4 days when pressed by the chicks running on it.

3. Two days before the chicks arrive, close all air and fan vents and close all windows. Set the electric bulbs at 8cm above the floor under the boxes. Use this for brooders.
4. Provide boxes in the room; 1 box for every 250 chicks.
5. Place a 60cm high surround of cardboard or hard board about 12 ft, 360cm in length around the brooder in cold weather but leave it on its own in the tropics.
6. Place 10 tabular feeder evenly inside the circular surround and press down firmly, each one in the litter.
7. Place (10 gallons), 50 litres troughs of water in the circle close to the center. If automatic drinkers are provided, they should be switched on one day after the chicks have arrived. But test them before hand.
8. On the remaining spaces, spread newspaper on the second day in the house, spread chick mash on the paper for the chicks to eat. That will be their third day from incubation.
9. Switch on all lights 48 hours before the chicks arrive.
10. Hang a minimum and maximum thermometer in the house to read the temperatures everyday.
11. When the heat is over 100 °F, open some windows to let some air in.
12. When the heat is below 60 °F, close the windows to raise the temperature.
13. When the chicks arrive, cull out the weak ones immediately.
14. Never open the boxes or release the chicks below a temperature of 60 °F (15 °C).
15. When a chick is warm, it will eat and drink, the rest is daily observation and reasoning.
16. Clean the drinkers and refill them daily.
17. On the 4th day, expand the surrounds (the enclosure of the cardboards).
18. Reduce the temperature slowly by opening one window at a time.
19. Remove newspaper spread on the wood shavings after 3 days.
20. Never fill feeders more than 2/3 full.

One percent of the chicks are bound to die. The good brooding and rearing methods laid down in this manual mean that at least 95% of those you have paid for as day old chicks will be fit to go into the laying house. You may lose another one percent during the laying period for unforeseen reasons.

All in all, you may have at most 90 out of every 100 chicks which will lay at their maximum. When some birds fail to lay, you should check these possible causes.

a. Nutrition defects- For nutrition defects, add cod liver oil to the feed at the rate of two tablespoonful to a bag (2kgs) of feed.
b. Disease- Check the appearance of the waste matter. Look for signs of coccidiosis which is signified by blood stained wastes. Provide dry litter and give Amprolium in the water. All Amprol drugs are effective.
c. Abnormality- Some cockrels have bodies like pullets. So be observant and cull (remove) them. Use Terramycin every two weeks to avoid any unexpected disease coming at production time.

CHAPTER 11: HOW TO PRESERVE EGGS AND SAVE MONEY

Eggs are one of the few available protein rich foods. Eggs constitute an important element in human nutrition. They replace meat in many homes and can be used in special diets for children and vegetarians.

Eggs can be used in numerous ways: boiled, fried or poached. Almost 95% of the people of the world enjoy eating eggs, and they are essential ingredient in cakes, puddings and savouries. Eggs should be one of the most important food reserves in the larder. The demand for eggs will rise from year to year because of the security of supply and to bigger population.

To take advantage of high prices and seasonal fluctuations, it is advisable to learn the techniques for preserving eggs in time of plenty and to ensure a constant and generous supply of eggs for home use. It takes skill, ingenuity and sound knowledge to preserve eggs perfectly. The quality of the eggs at the end of the preserving period depends mainly on the care given to their selection for preservation.

For perfect preservation result, pay attention to the following rules:

1. Eggs to be preserved should not be more than 24 hours old after laying.
2. Eggs should be free from cracks.
3. Eggs should have strong, unspotted shells.
4. Soft and thin shelled eggs should not be preserved.
5. Eggs should be clean.
6. Eggs should never be washed with water, because the shell is porous.
7. Do not deep freeze eggs because the contents will expand and crack the shell. Egg contains about 60 % of water, and on freezing, water increases in volume.
8. Store preserved eggs in a cool, airy place.
9. Store the eggs in a container with a lid. Cover the egg with wax paper or aluminium foil before the lid is put on tight.
10. Before boiling any fresh or preserved egg, puncture the large end with a pin to let the air out and to prevent the shell from cracking in the hot water.
11. Preserved eggs are perhaps better fried or scrambled in case of doubt about their condition.

PERFECT METHODS FOR THE PRESERVATION OF EGGS

A. BY BUTTER: The easiest method of preserving eggs for short periods is to smear them with butter. The egg shell is porous and permeable to liquid. Therefore, only good fresh butter should be used. The eggs also must be fresh.

PROCEDURE:

1. Rub a small quantity of butter in your palm.
2. Place the fresh egg in one palm and put the other palm on top of the egg between the two palms, making sure that the entire shell is covered with butter.
3. Stand the buttered eggs upwards and store them in a cool place. They will stay fresh for two months.

B. USING LARD AND BORIC POWDER

1. Buy a lard and boric powder. Cream together 2 parts of lard and 1 part boric powder (boracic acid).

2. Cover evenly one egg at a time with a thin layer of the mixture.
3. Cover the whole shell and repeat the process until every egg is covered.
4. Place the eggs in a tray with the narrow end down and the broad end up.
5. Keep the eggs in a box or on a tray with a good air circulation.
6. Store in a cool dry place with plenty of air.
7. The eggs stay fresh for a maximum of two months. Gently roll the egg.

C. BY SILICATE OF SODA.

This method has proved to be the most effective. The recommended solution is (1lb) of silicate of soda (water glass) to 1 gallon of water, i.e. 50g to 5litres of water is (1/2 kg to 5 litres). Perhaps the best preservative solution is a weaker mixture of (1lb), ½ kg of silicate of soda to (1 ½ gallons) 7 ½ litres of water.

PROCEDURE:

1. Add the (water glass), silicate of soda to boiling water.
2. Thoroughly mix together by stirring.
3. Leave the solution to cool. The end result is the preservative.
4. Keep the solution in a bucket.
5. Place the fresh eggs in the preservative within the first day of laying.
6. Put about 120 eggs (10 dozen) in a big bucket or trough of the preservative.
7. The top layer of the eggs should be 1 inch (2.5cm) below the surface of the preservative liquid. The eggs will be preserved for as long as it takes (to sell them).

D. BY LIME WATER
1. Mix (2 ½ lb) 1.25 kg of fresh slake lime in (5 gallons) 22.5 litres of cold, clean water.
2. Stir the mixture frequently until it dissolves.
3. Allow to settle for 12 hours.
4. Pour off the clean liquid from the top.
5. This forms the preservatives.
6. Collect several dozen eggs and dip them in the preservative liquid.
7. This will preserve the eggs for as long as it takes (to sell them).

E. WHOLE EGGS BY DEEP FREEZING
1. Break a few eggs into a boil and whisk slightly.

2. Add ½ teaspoon of salt or 2 tablespoon of sugar.
3. Pour into separate plastic bags and store in a deep freezer.

CHAPTER 12: BROILERS, ANOTHER MONEY SPINNER

Broilers are young chickens weighing between (2 ½ - 4 ½ lbs) 1-2 kgs live weight. Broilers are fast growing special chickens reared for meat. Most of them are sold at the age of 54 weeks and this makes them, the most profitable venture in any business.

Their bodies are more meaty with little bones. Broilers reach between (3-4 lbs) 1.4-1.8 kgs from 8 ¾ to 10 weeks. There should be space in a deep litter house with plenty of space so that they are comfortable.

In order to get the greatest profit from broilers, there is a new secret called " The co-operative method" . Start the day old broiler chicks batches with one month interval. Big commercial farms can use a 2-3 weeks interval. Where cardboard surrounds are used, they should be moved after 7 days.

A. ORGANISED PRODUCTION

You need 3 separate buildings, but 2 buildings will do, depending upon the quantity of the birds. The first house is for brooders, the second for rearing and the third is the grower and marketing house. In the brooder house, spread fresh litter material- saw dust, sand, wood shavings or rice husk fibres- on the floor of the house. Cool sand should be 2 cm deep and dry and other litter should be 3 inches (8cm) deep.

Prepare the room in the same way as for the other chicks. Disinfect for 3 weeks before the new day -old chicks arrive . Serve water in clean , covered containers (troughs) 24 hours before the birds arrive. Give them plenty of water. They need water exactly as any other day old chicks.

A temperature of 95 °F is needed in the day old chick broilers room. Bring this temperature down after 4 weeks.

Open some of the windows after week 4. If the chicks crowd together, it is a sign that they are having cold. If they crowd against the wall and the door, it is a sign that they are very hot. This indicates that you should open all the windows and doors.

Debeak the chicks after 1 week. Provide red bulb light of any kind to prevent fighting and cannibalism among the birds.

Bring the temperature down by using lower density electric bulbs. The lower the heat density, the less the fighting amongst the poultry.

FEEDING METHODS.

Only 2 types of feed should be used.

1. Never make your own broiler mash. Leave that to the experts. Feed the broilers, starter's mash between 1 day and 4 weeks old.
2. On 4 weeks, move the birds to another room if necessary.
3. From week 5, feed the birds on only broiler finisher mash. They live on this feed until the 14th week when they are sold.
4. Many times a day, from a day-old, give water and feed.
5. Water must be regular and on time. Broilers are not like ordinary chicks, they do not like to miss their food and water from a day-old to 7 days.
6. Spread the feed on newspaper on top of the litter.
a. Suppose you produce 100 broilers for each sale per month, in one year, 12 months, you sell 1,200 broilers and if they are each sold at $4, then 1,200 x 4 = $4,800. That is $4, 800 income in one year from your hobby. As for your costs, in 14 weeks, your 500 birds will eat $490 worth of feed.
In one year, there will be 3 groups, so 490 x 3 = $1, 470 worth of feed. This means that your net profit from $1,200 broilers in one year will be $14, 530; ($4,800- $1, 470).
b. Increase the number of birds and you increase your profit margin. One small scale business man has 3 houses, each containing 1,000 broilers, so there is a total of 3,000 broilers selling at $4 each. 3,000x 4 = $12,000 in every sale time . But remember that there are 3 sales in a year , so income is $12,000 x 3 = $36,000 (Thirty six thousand dollars) per year.
c. Suppose you decide to go into it professionally and build 5 houses. If each house contains 1,000 broilers , then 1,000 x 5 =5,000 broilers at each sale. In one year, you will have 3 sales, so 5,000 x 3= 15,000 broilers each year. If

you sell each broiler at $3, you get 15,000 x 4 = $60,000 a year income. In the poultry business, the sky is the only limit. You can make as much money as you like. You only need a little care and to follow systematically the guide laid down in this manual, step by step.

CHAPTER 13: BROILERS – MAXIMUM EFFICIENCY

Maximum efficiency is rather difficult if several age groups are in one house together. Diseases build up easily and spread faster from older to younger birds. It is both advisable and profitable to rear your broilers in age groups. Suitable types of chicks are essential for different broiler production. Buy your day-old chicks from good private firms if possible. The following birds grow faster: HUBBARD,

COBB, PILCH, AND HYBRID. Local and foreign cross breeds produce excellent growth.

1. Birds should be fast growers, better and efficient food converters.
2. They should have good breast width and be neat.
3. They should be fast feathering to prevent feather-pecking.
4. They should have yellow feet in the tropics and pale/white feet in temperate regions.
5. The parents should be good egg-layers, with over 240 eggs per season. The progeny of the above poultry are fast growers.

FEED COMPOSITION

Special broiler rations are needed so that each can grow faster and convert food efficiently. Fast growing broiler chickens require a higher level of energy, protein, vitamins and minerals than the level required by pullets and other chickens intended for egg production. Do not feed ordinary chicken rations to the broilers and expect good result. A typical broiler ration may consist of 65% high energy, flour, tapioca (yellow maize) and 35% protein. Add vitamin K and D, as well as small amount of the following:

a. Green vegetables.
b. Minerals.
c. Antibiotics.
d. Dried yeast.
e. Vitamin E (methionine)
f. Lard- This increases the energy content of the ration (antioxidant).

Feed starter ration up to the age of 35 days before you change to finisher ration.

HOUSING

A special broiler house is necessary for only large broiler unit. Any building can be converted to suit the purpose. Broiler houses should measure (4 ½ to 5 ft) 135- 150 cm to the ends and (10 ft), 500 cm from floor level to the cage. Flour space per bird is chicks (6 sq. ins) 15sq.cm and adults (1sq ft) 30 sq .cm per bird. For good results, broilers need a well ventilated house.

If the temperature is lower than the normal 90 °F level, then use then the chickens will need extra feed to keep up their body heat. Use corrugated iron for roofing as this repels most of the heat. Asbestors retain the heat for longer periods.

MANAGEMENT FOR PROFIT

In commercial broiler production, the producer must be well versed in the care and management of chicks. Before taking on a broiler project, it is desirable that experience and skill be obtained on an existing unit which is profitably run. Anybody trained to care for ordinary chicks can look after broiler chicks.

However, large commercial numbers brooded together have some perculiar and certain special requirement. Always check and put fresh litter near the drinkers to cover up the wet areas, because wet litter increases the incidence of diseases. Change the litter between each batch to get rid of coccidiosis and roundworm eggs. Where fresh litter is expensive to obtain, you can use the old litter several times provided you follow these instructions. Heap the old litter for 3-6 hours to heat up, then spread it again by carefully turning it over.

ROUTINE DAILY CARE

A clear watch must be kept on the broilers so that any sudden setback in growth can be noticed at once.

1. The first setback sign is a reduction in water intake. When water consumption is less, expect some trouble, illness or diseases.
2. Less feed intake is another sign of danger.
3. Setbacks may be due to coccidiosis, roundworms, deficiencies in food, bad ventilation or pneumonia.
4. Experienced poultry farmers will notice from their experience of the birds, if they are developing sickness.
5. Give extra antibiotics such as terramycin poultry formular to prevent disease.

6. Identify the actual sickness/ disease and prescribe a proper drug. Antibiotics do not remedy some diseases.
7. Feather pecking is overcome by dim lights or red bulbs.
8. Inadequate feeding, inadequate water or drinking space and unbalanced rations all lead to stress. Stress leads to feather pecking which leads to cannibalism and reduce growth.
9. Dust , cobwebs and fluff should not be allowed to remain in the rooms.
10. Scrape all old food and any caked material from food troughs.
11. As a routine, all fittings and the floor should be soaked and scrubbed with 4% solution of hypochlorite. Add some detergent in the solution (Hypochlorite and $HClO_3$ from household bleach).
12. To cure Coccidiosis disease, wash the floor again with 10% solution of Ammonia. Ammonia is dangerous , so wear a mask on your nose when in the chicken house.
13. You can use Izal as a detergent in the chicken house.
14. If a severe and dangerous outbreak of disease occurs, disinfect the house. Stream hot water will do.
15. Mix potassium permanganate and formalin to generate formalin gas in the room. Only 20 g of formalin is required per cubic meter and 2 fluid ounces per 100 cubic feet on buildings of 1200 cubic feet (340 cubic meters).

WARNING: Potassium permanganate and formalin compounds react violently , if mixed incorrectly. Be careful when mixing them. When the disease outbreak has occurred, remove litter and burn it. Soak the room (If not cemented) in 1 pint (0.5 litres) of formalin to 15 gallons (75 litres) of potassium permanganate solution. Let all the houses rest for 2 weeks after treatment.

CHAPTER 14: TURNING HOBBY INTO BUSINESS: STARTING 1,000 BROILERS OR MORE.

HOUSE AND EQUIPMENT: This is what you need to avoid problems.

1. One house of (750 sq. ft.) 70 sq.m. floor area is needed.
2. About 1000 broiler day-old chicks are needed.
3. Shut all windows and fix lights in the house.
4. Cardboard- Surround or any box can be used for their protection against panic.
5. Red bulbs fixed at 8 cm high above the ground are needed.
6. 10 drinkers: (1 gallon) 4.5 litres are needed.
7. 6 drinkers: (6ft) 1.8 cm size accessible from all sides of the room must be provided.
8. 36-40 tabular feeders: (3 inches) 76 cm of trough per bird are needed.
9. A concrete bunker 90 x 90x 60 cm must be built outside the poultry house to sink the troughs in.

FOOD NEEDED

1. 1 ½ ton (1.27) broiler starter feed (crumbs)

2. 3 ½ ton (3.2 tonnes) broiler mash (pellet).
3. 50 lb (25kg) chicken size sand (granite grit) if desired.

PROCEDURE

1. Clean and disinfect the house before and after use.
2. Leave the house to rest 2 weeks after cleaning.
3. Place (4 inches) 10 cm of litter (wood shaving, sand etc) on the floor.
4. Put light on 48 hours and set water out 24 hours before the chicks arrive.
5. Close all the windows for the first 7 days and open them all after 4 weeks.
6. Give only water to the chicks on the 2nd day and feed on the 3rd day.
7. Put the chicks feed on paper during the first 4 days.
8. Inspect the birds at night after they have settled down to sleep.
9. Open one window at a time after 7 days.
10. Change feeders gradually at the end of the first 7 days.
11. Keep feeders half–full.
12. Remove and scrub caked feed from troughs.
13. Inspect the chickens often- every morning and every time you feed them.
14. Check and note feed consumed by the chicks per day and per week.

EFFICIENT PRODUCTION METHODS

Maximum efficiency is essential to make a huge profit from broilers and to allow for increased production for the market. Maximum efficiency comes from proper breeding, good quality chicks, balanced rations, housing and above all SKILLED MANAGEMENT. Where these factors are combined to the credit of the poultry manager, excellent result is the outcome. The combination brings:

1. Low production costs.
2. Profit are high even at low market prices.
3. The results are measured by the live weight of the birds and less food consumption.
4. The food conversion rate becomes the best in the business.
5. Turnover is very rapid (only 14 weeks).
6. Even a small profit per bird (live weight) gives high overall profit return on the money invested.

7. Much of the profit depends on feed management, efficiency of food conversion and live weight. Live weight is part and parcel of food conversion and yet the two vary completely. Both depend on the efficiency of the poultry man and his ability, skill and success in applying the principles outlined in this manual.
8. If mortality is kept at a low rate and other costs are fixed, then half the battle is won.
9. Labour costs are very low compared with feeding costs. The cost of a skilled poultry man is repaid in short term, so seek labour efficiency rather than mere knowledge of poultry.

CHAPTER 15: REARING LARGER COCKERELS FOR PROFIT

In tropical countries, it is far economical to produce cockerels for festive occasions than for market. To produce profitable cockerels, attention should be paid mostly to their sizes and weight which should be far greater than those of hens of the same age. The weight of a proper fully grown cockrel is much more than that of broilers. The average broiler weight is (3 ½ or 4lb) 2kg . To achieve this required standard, you should endeavor to adopt intensive methods throughout the 14 weeks of their lives. Broilers are marketed at 14 weeks of age. The intensive method is not abundantly essential as there are other alternative methods.

You can achieve the same maximum weight on free range and on semi-intensive means. What is important is to hatch your chicks at appropriate time, so that they attain the required weight for Christmas among Christians and Sallah in the Moslem world. These periods and others like Easter are market boom period. Get prepared and be ready for them.

COCKERELS

Cockerels of good stock easily reach their live weight of (8 lb) 4kg when they are 20 weeks old. They should then be sold to compensate for the extra fee required for pullets entering the laying house. Cockerels should not be retained beyond the age of 20 weeks when they are in intensive care. If your cockerels are on free range , you can leave them alone to feed themselves in the farm. Cockerels intended to reach a certain market should be batched 20 weeks before.

For example, for Christmas sales, the chicks on the free range farm as cockerels are to be hardened in the previous June. For example, for Christmas sales, the chicks on the free range farm as cockerels are to be hardened in the previous June. For example, you may decide to use your garage of 750 – 300 cm (25 x 10 ft), this gives 7, 500 cm on (2, 000 sq/ft x 20) 500 day-old. If the birds are to be placed in the intensive litter house, then they should be hatched in July in order to fulfill the Christmas needs. The Moslem world have festive seasons which falls in August and October almost every year.

FEEDING

It is advisable to feed the cockerels on special diet first because the diet helps to produce more rapid growth. The standard, normal chick mash should be fed to the chicken / cockrels for 8 weeks . This is essential and after that age continue with grower mash.

CHAPTER 16: SUMMARY OF POULTRY MANAGEMENT SCIENCE

When you are starting poultry, the most important thing to do is to choose your room. Prepare the room with timber shavings before the spread of the litter. The number of day-old chicks needed should be thought of . To know how many you need, just measure the room length and breath for 15sq. cm per bird.

For example, you may decide to use your garage for 2,700 birds. Out of the number, 10% are expected to die which is about 270 birds. The remaining number can stay in the garage until after their laying period.

Table 3: Production all the year round table

HATCHING DATE	CHICKS	MARKETING BROILERS	MARKETING COCKERELS	LAYERS	FULL PRODUCTION
January	February	April	June	June	June - November
February	March	May	July	July	July- December
March	April	June	August	August	August- January
April	May	July	September	September	September – February.
May	June	August	October	October	October - March
June	July	September	November	November	November- April
July	August	October	December	December	December - May
August	September	November	January	January	January -June
September	October	December	February	February	February - July
October	November	January	March	March	March – August
November	December	February	April	April	April- September
December	January	March	May	May	May- October
Day -olds	4 weeks	12 weeks	20 weeks	52 weeks	12-15 weeks

NOTE: These times and periods are not static. Some January chicks may lay their first eggs in May rather than June. The growing period does not start and end within 12 weeks. Rather it is continuous from the day of hatching until the end of the season. These names are given only for identification of periods. There is a resting period before the 12th month, which is the starting point of the second laying season.

The whole life cycle of the hen stops at the end of the second season, 15 months in the tropics, but in temperate countries, an extra 2 weeks is added.

In temperate regions of the world , the hen stops laying at 52 weeks , while in tropical countries , the period is 72 weeks. Depending on the lighting programme recommended in this manual, peak production will be as follows:

1. Hot/ dry regions ; 50 % eggs laid at 30- 36 weeks old.
2. Colder places ; 90% eggs laid at 25- 30 weeks old.

Maturity age of 50% production is 30- 36 weeks of age in the tropics and 25 -30 weeks in temperate .

PREPARING TO RECEIVE THEM

After the wood shavings are spread on the room, cover the floor , over the top of the litter with old newspapers. A day before the spread of the litter , down wash and disinfect the room with any disinfectant i.e. Dettol or Izal.

When you finish spreading the paper on the floor, keep the water in the troughs . Every 100 chicks will need 5 litres of water (1 gallon of water) . This troughs should be spaced at 90 cm (3ft) from the wall and from one another. The water must be in the room 24 hours before the chicks arrive. The next are lighting which should be either in the ceiling or on the wall at 9 to 10 ft. (300 cm) apart.

A BROODER BOX.

This is a box with the opposite end open and a hole at the other end . A 25 watt bulb is fixed inside the box. The box should be supported on hinges (3m) 5 cm from the litter. Preferably , red bulb are used under the boxes. There is no specific size for a brooder box but it should be spacious enough for the birds.

CHAPTER 16: COMMON POULTRY DISEASES

1. ASPERGILLOSIS: This is a fungus from wet food, contaminated water and old food which affects the respiratory tract and causes pneumonia. Its mortality rate is 50% among chicks and 55% in pullets. For prevention, avoid mouldy litter and maintain good overall hygiene. This is very important.

2. SALMONELLOSIS (BWD): Bacillary white diarrhea is a killer. The waste of the bird is watery with watery white at the edge. It is hereditary. Prevent it by good hygiene and sanitation practice. Kill odour in the chicken house.

Whitish sticky droppings block the vent causing death from day 1- 3 weeks . In pot belly chicks, use furazolidone.

3. WORMS: For worms , the treatment is with piperazine compound. It is very effective against large round worms.
4. CANNIBALISM: It starts from stress , lack of feed, and too high a temperature in the room . The immediate cause is pecking which leads directly to cannibalism. Hang red electric bulb, 5 cm above the ground in the house to stop cannibalism among the birds. Use any red light.
5. FOWL TYPHOID: It is a very contagious disease among poultry. It originated and was discovered in East Africa Kikuyu area. It is called Kikuyu fowl disease in East Africa. The same disease is internationally known as the second disease. The bird becomes sleepy, loses appetite but becomes very thirsty, though it refuses to drink.

The sick bird stands with the head close to its body. The comb strands of male bird becomes pale and dark in severe case. The best symptom is that the bird passes liquid , greenish – yellow droppings.

Such birds die from 2 to 6 days. The sickness is infectious to other poultry. Until now, there has been no effective cure except to burn the dead bird.

The Chinese have come to our aid with FURADIS 25 (See Module 17). Furazolidon in water does the same work. Fowl typhoid is an acute disease among poultry and causes considerable losses. It is associated with bad hygiene. It can be brought into the house by a carrier bird through the droppings which contaminate the ground, houses, litter, feed and water. It is often brought in by mice and rats. It comes through sudden changes of weather.

SIGNS: The fowl becomes sharpy and dull with the breed down into the body. The feathers ruffle and comb and wattles becomes dark red or light red in colour. The birds feel intense thirst but refuse to drink.

SYMPTOMS : There is a passage of stinking liquid droppings of sulphur- yellow or greenish-yellow colour . Mortality is 50%.

PREVENTION: Vaccinate against fowl typhoid at 6 months old.

CONTROL: All sick birds should be removed and the remainder of the birds given Sulphaquinoline in water or Furazoline in feed. Germs are destroyed by spray disinfectant. Furazoline is effective.

6. OMPHALITIS: This is an incubator disease. It is a navel infection caused by faulty incubation temperature. Death is within the first 7 days. Treatment is not necessary as death is inevitable.
7. LIVER – KIDNEY SYNDROME (PINK DISEASE): Pink disease is the common name. The autopsy shows the liver and kidney to be infected.

TREATMENT: Starvation for the first 2 days and plenty of water helps to stop the disease. Autopsy show a heavy disposition of the liver due to stress.

8. EPIDEMIC TREMORS: This disease is caused from the egg and mildly infects the day old chicks. It erupts in week 23-24 and is a killer disease. Prevention is with antibiotics between weeks 20 and 22. An approved vaccine against the breeding stock is satisfactory.
9. JOINTS: Lameness and swollen joints may be due to nutritional problems. It may also be due to an infection such as Staphylococcus and /or mycoplasma. When it is a nutritional problem , then add cod liver oil to the feed. When it is due to infection, then the treatment is Aureomycine or Terramycin at a low level of 100g per ton of feed. Bandage the joint to give support.
10. NUTRITIONAL DISORDER: Unbalanced feed causes crazy chick disease, rickets, perosis (slipped tender), swollen socks, retarded growth and poor feathering. Limestone grit should be not be added to the feed composition. Give more protein feed e.g. Soya beans and leaves.
11. FEATHER AND SKIN PECKING: Feather pecking is common among birds in close confinement. It is caused by ONE WAY FEED. It is also caused by too much starch in the feed. It may also be caused by lack of other feed ingredients e.g. Vitamins and or minerals.
TREATMENT:

1. Provide green feed, dust the birds with sodium fluoride or a mixture of wood ash and sulphur.
2. The affected part of the bird should be treated with sulphur and petroleum jelly, Oil or Vaseline.
3. Increase the minerals in the feed.
4. Add cod liver oil in the feed by all means for 10 days.

12. SCALY LEGS: The scales on the legs of the birds actually are seen raised with some white rust in the legs. The legs appear to bleed. It is caused by white ants which make holes on the legs and under the scales. The disease appears where birds are raised under insanitary conditions.

TREATMENT

1. Use an ointment with same amount of sulphur powder on the affected legs.
2. In severe cases; dip the affected leg in paraffin(kerosene).

13. WHITE COMBE DISEASE: It is a fungus disease which spreads on the comb and in the feathers.

TREATMENT:

1. Use warm water and sulphur ointment for treatment.
2. Use 5% of silver nitrate in Vaseline cream at the affected parts.
3. Again, in the absence of the above treatment, use natural lime fruit. Squeeze the lime juice on the affected parts and ribs three times in one week.

NOTE: This fungus is infectious to people, so be careful. Use gloves and wash your hands afterward.

14. FOWL CHOLERA: The infectious germs develop from 2 hours to 3 days. In many cases, one does not notice any sign of illness before the birds suddenly die. The common sign is whitish watery discharge from nose, mouth and eyes. At the point of death, the birds fall down on their sides and die struggling. In general, some birds show the following signs:

1. Loose appetite.
2. Feel great taste.
3. Dropping of head, wings and tail feather pointing downwards.

4. Swinging from side to side (like a drunkard).
5. Quick and short breath but experience difficulty in breathing.
6. Whitish yellowish dropping are common.
7. Droppings are watery and sticky.

NOTE: No matter what, the affected birds will surely die. More often than not, 80%- 90% of the affected birds die.

MEDICINE: Furadis 25.

PREVENTION: All affected birds should be isolated for 14 days before allowed to join the group, should such birds survive.

15. CONTAGIOUS CATTARR:

SIGNS:

1. The affected bird sneezes often and breaths through its mouth wide open.
2. It often shakes its head.
3. The face puffs up.
4. The sickness is contagious to other birds.
5. The liquid in the mouth and nostrils dry up.

NOTE: Fortunately, this sickness does not kill.

PREVENTION: Increase your supply of vegetables in feed to the birds. Give the birds some raw cabbage and carrots to pick and eat. Add a little iodine into the drinking water of the birds.

16. NEWCASTLE DISEASE: Two symptoms are evident.
1. Respiratory disease. Layers drop production, poor shell egg are produced. Moulting and green diarrhea are common.
2. Nervous distress with high mortality.

CHAPTER 17: ESTABLISHED POULTRY MEDICATION AND VACCINES.

The following list gives the established drugs to be given for various diseases.

- A. COCCIDIOSIS
    1. Amprolium
    2. Sulphatimidine
    3. Suphaquinoxaline.
    4. Nitroturaze.
- B. INFECTIOUS BRONCHITIS
    1. Tylan
    2. Terramycin Chick Formular.
    3. Terramycin Egg Formular.
    4. Furagalli.
- C. STRESS
    1. Solinster stress
    2. Furagalli.
- D. ANTIBIOTICS
    1. Euraviste.
    2. Terramycin poultry formular.
    3. Floxaid.

NOTE: One packet (1 sachet) for 100 litres, (22 gallons) of water for 4 to 5 days for complete cure and eradication of the disease. The following list gives new poultry drugs:

1. AUREOMYCIN: This is a day old chick drug. Aureomycin soluble powder in the drinking water is for broad disease coverage. You as a poultry man

cannot afford disease to strike your chicks and lose important profits. Day old-chicks need the early protection of Aureomycin chlorotetracycline in drinking water on the first day. It keeps poultry healthy and prevents chronic respiratory disease (C.R.D) or air sac disease. The Aureomycin soluble powder for better feed efficiency and weight is given. Blue comb and most poultry infections are treated with Aureomycin.

2. NOVASTAT: This is a broiler drug. It is effective against all economically strains of Coccidia. Broilers make full use of their feed and perform better at a lower cost. Novastat, when combined with 3 Nitro, Novastat helps to improve it. Diseases is reduced.
3. POULAC VACCINES: This is good for Newcastle disease, Fowl pox infections and bronchitis. It is safe for broilers.
4. SPECTAM (SPECTANOMYCIN): It is a safe antibiotic which prevents chronic respiratory diseases (C.R.D) and Fowl cholera.
5. FERMACTO 500 : Use Fermacto 500 or other similar additives for broiler feed supplement. It produces greater live weight gain for broilers, turkeys and high egg production for layers.

A NOTE ON CRACKED EGGS

In cages where cracked eggs are a problem, pay attention to the slope of the wires and also the sloped floor of the house. It is not disease or birds which crack the eggs. Check up all your farm equipment.

6. FURADIS 25: This is a Chinese poultry medicine. Instructions are written in Chinese language. It is a general purpose medicine and one of the best in the market. It prevents most of the diseases known in tropical poultry. It also cures major acute illness in poultry, if properly applied. Unfortunately, all instruction are written in Chinese.

NOTES: FURADIS; INSTRUCTIONS TO USE FOR CURE

One tea spoonful in 5 litres of water or two teaspoonful per 2 gallons or 10 litres of water. For prevention: One teaspoon of Furadis 25 in 10 litres of water.

CHAPTER 18 : APPLICATION OF POULTRY VACCINES

1. VACCINE STORAGE: Newcastle intraocular (N.D.V.L) at 40 °C.

RECONSTITUTION : For 200 dose Ampol , dissolve in 10 ml of Saline. Use immediately in drinking water.

DOSE: One drop into eye. Use dropping nozzle 0.02 ml per dose.

AGE: One day old.

DURATION: 30 months.

2. VACCINE STORAGE: Newcastle ; 1 year at 40 o C (N.D.V.L).

RECONSTITUTION:For 50 and 200 dose Ampol , dissolve in 10 ml of chlorine. Fresh water for each bird. 2.5 ml skimmed milk cai be added to each litre of water. Use immediately. (See week 4).

DOSE: Allow 10 ml of water for each bird. Make birds thirsty by removing drinking water.

AGE: Any age , every 3 weeks.

DURATION: 6 months.

3. VACCINE STORAGE: Newcastle ; 1 year (N.D.V.L) at 40 °C.
4. RECONSTRUCTION: For 50- 200 dose Ampol , dissolve in 2ml and 8 ml distilled water or normal saline respectively. Use immediately.

DOSE: By stab inoculation in wing web. Two stabs on each wing.

AGE: Preferably over 3-6 weeks. One vaccination is sufficient. Examine and observe birds 7- 10 days after vaccination. Provide drinking water for several hours.

For further information on step by step guide for profitable poultry farming for local production and export or sources of agricultural loans, please contact:

PHILIP NELSON INSTITUTE OF AGRICULTURAL RESEARCH.

Telephone: +2348166582414, +2348140624643, +2348173175179.

E-mail: philipnelsoninstitute@yahoo.com

www.ingramcontent.com/pod-product-compliance
Lightning Source LLC
Chambersburg PA
CBHW021500210526
45463CB00002B/825